Harold Nelson Burden

Manitoulin : or, Five Years of Church Work Among Ojibway Indians

And Lumbermen, Resident upon that Island or in its Vicinity

Harold Nelson Burden

Manitoulin : or, Five Years of Church Work Among Ojibway Indians
And Lumbermen, Resident upon that Island or in its Vicinity

ISBN/EAN: 9783744722421

Printed in Europe, USA, Canada, Australia, Japan

Cover: Foto ©Lupo / pixelio.de

More available books at **www.hansebooks.com**

MANITOULIN;

OR,

Five Years of Church Work among Ojibway Indians and Lumbermen, resident upon that Island or in its Vicinity.

BY

H. N. B.

AN ASSISTANT COLLEGE CHAPLAIN AT CAMBRIDGE,

Licensed Priest in the Province of Canterbury, Liveryman and Citizen of London, and Fellow of the Royal Society of Literature. Author of "Uffington Notes," "Life in Algoma," etc.

AT ALL LIBRARIES AND BOOKSELLERS IN TOWN AND COUNTRY.

LONDON:
SIMPKIN, MARSHALL, HAMILTON, KENT & Co., LTD.
1895.

THIS LITTLE BOOK IS DEDICATED

TO A NAME

TOO REVERED AND TOO DEAR FOR ME TO ATTEMPT

TO SAY OF IT WHAT I WOULD,

EDWARD,

LORD BISHOP OF ALGOMA,

IN ACKNOWLEDGMENT OF MANY BLESSINGS, AND OF HIS

GREAT SYMPATHY, BOTH, WHILE I WAS ONE OF HIS

CLERGY, AND SINCE MY REMOVAL FROM THAT DIOCESE,

TO PATHS OF DUTY IN THIS GREAT UNIVERSITY.

THE AUTHOR.

CONTENTS.

Chapter		Page
	Preface	7
	Author's Preface	13
I.	Introduction	15
II.	Early Days	21
III.	Sheguiandah	27
IV.	Christmas	34
V.	Bad Travelling	39
VI.	Indian Superstitions	46
VII.	An Ice Accident	52
VIII.	The Evangeline	59
IX.	The Bishop's Arrival	66
X.	A Heavy Day's Work	71
XI.	An Indian Picnic	77
XII.	Aundagwahmenekauning	84
XIII.	Spring	90
XIV.	An Episcopal Visitation	97
XV.	Delays	104
XVI.	Gore Bay	110
XVII.	Birch Island	115
XVIII.	Burnt Out	124
XIX.	An Indian Funeral	131
XX.	Saw Mills	136
XXI.	Among Lumbermen	143
XXII.	A Wedding	150
XXIII.	Conclusion	155

ILLUSTRATIONS.

A Jam of Logs	*Frontispiece.*	
The Lord's Prayer in Ojibway	Facing Page	14
Map of the Manitoulin Island	,, ,,	16
Sheguiandah Church	,, ,,	28
A Load of Logs	,, ,,	42
The Evangeline	,, ,,	56
An Indian Picnic	,, ,,	78
The Rev. F. Frost Travelling	,, ,,	90
Portaging	,, ,,	100
Little Current Lumber Yard	,, ,,	118
A Wigwam	,, ,,	128
A Saw Mill	,, ,,	138
Lumbermen	,, ,,	146
In Journeyings oft	,, ,,	161

PREFACE.

"Fancy suggesting that any lake in North America contains an "island over one hundred miles long where the ice bridge is in "winter the only means of access to the mainland twenty miles "off! The atlas shows no such dimensions for any of the *few* "islands lying in Lake Huron."

Such was the reply of an old gentleman, who brought an antiquated atlas with him to prove me mistaken, when I mentioned these facts to stir up his sympathies, and get him to contribute clothing and magazines towards the box I was about to pack, and send to the Bishop of Algoma, for the benefit of dwellers on the great Manitoulin.

"Indeed, but I am speaking the truth," I said, "and if you "look at a recent official atlas, you will find the area of Mani-"toulin Island such as I describe. You will also find innu-"merable islands scattered throughout the two hundred miles "between Saulte Ste Marie in the West, and Parry Sound in "the East." In the Georgian Bay alone, Commander Wakefield noted 27,000.

In Spring and Autumn the islanders are cut off from the mainland for weeks at a time, by reason of shifting ice. In summer they travel by boat or canoe, and the steamers of the Great Northern Company call twice a week at points on the islands, and stations on the opposite mainland across the inside channel.

As an example of a winter journey between mainland and island, I quote the experience of a missionary, then in charge of Algoma Mills.

"Mr. G. re-crossed the frozen channel more than twenty miles

"in width, in the teeth of a blinding snowstorm, with the thermo-
" meter so low that several lives were lost on the same day, not
" far from the route he took ; while he himself was so crippled by
" the intense cold, that though he had bread in his wallet, his
" hands refused their office, unable to raise it to his mouth, and
" he was compelled to drop it on the snow, and go on his way,
" famishing with hunger, in hope of reaching his destination at
" Blind River. This, however, he missed by two or three miles,
" striking a point to the east, where the only shelter to be found
" was a deserted fishing shanty. Here he passed the night,
" without fire, light, or blankets, resuming his journey in the
" morning, astonishing his friends by his unexpected appearance
" in their midst. Weary and exhausted as he must have been,
" he resisted all their entreaties to lie down and get a few hours
" sleep, contenting himself with a quiet rest till evening, when
" he held service and once more delivered his Master's message."

I once wrote to the late clergyman of Gore Bay enquiring in his district would be a good locality for emigration. I insert his reply, thinking it may be of general interest and give a peep at the life of the neighbourhood.

"You can form an idea of the want of religious influences in
" new settlements, when one clergyman (as in this mission) has
" to work single-handed over some 700 square miles of territory,
" while, 'beyond the hills' there are people who may be said
" never to see the face of a clergyman from one year to another
" Of course, as these regions become peopled, efforts will be
" made to supply them with the ministrations of religion. Still,
" for all the drawbacks inseparable from new settlements, the
" wonder is that thousands in the overcrowded districts of the
" old country do not come out here.

" The ordinary settler's house is built of logs, either hewn flat
" on two sides, or left in the round, and their houses or huts are
" eighteen by twenty-four feet. The work of this mission is hard,
" sometimes dangerous, but always encouraging.

"I might mention for instance, how I have been caught on
"the open ice in "blizzards" (heavy snow-storms) and have had
"to travel for miles without being able to see ten feet in any
"direction, and having to trust to the sagacity of my horse to
"bring me safely through. I could mention being forced to lie
"on the beach all night without food or shelter, not being able
"to face the waves in my open boat. I could mention how I
"travelled on New Year's Eve for twenty-four miles over roads,
"sometimes covered with ice and water, from two to three feet
"in depth, for a quarter of a mile at a stretch.

"When I came to open up this mission about four years ago,
"I found that the people were fast becoming atheists, and all
"manner of scepticism was to be met with, which was the result
"of the absence of Church teaching. But things are changed
"now. The strange notions which the people had adopted have
"mostly been given up for better things; they have learned
"to speculate in religion less, and to read their Bibles more;
"and wherever the Church's standard has been planted there
"has sprung up religious life and activity, in place of the old
"spiritual deadness and indifference. Already three churches
"have been built in this mission, and more will be undertaken
"before very long.

"Your letter came to hand a few days before Christmas
"together with the books, cards and mottoes. Their arrival was
"most opportune, as we were getting up a Sunday School
"Christmas festival, and were hard pressed for materials.
"Through the medium of the Christmas tree, the beautiful
"cards and mottoes have been distributed all through the
"mission and the recipients appeared greatly delighted. The
"prettily bound books and most of the testaments were dis-
"tributed at the same time, the latter going to the more
"deserving children; and we were enabled through this help
"to present every Sunday School child with a useful and
"attractive gift."

B

PREFACE.

These letters were dated 1884. It is now 1895, and notwithstanding all his efforts to obtain additional clergy the Bishop of Algoma has now only the same number of ordained missionaries for that portion of his diocese, as when those words were written.

In a sermon preached during 1893 the Bishop spoke of *our* responsibilities to assist the emigrants to obtain the ministrations of our Church.

"Most of these people are your own. They speak your "language, are attached to your throne and constitution, many "of them are your own relations and friends. They need the "same crucified Saviour of whom we have been speaking. You "have sent them in a destitute condition from your shores. "Canada has relieved you of the burden and given every family "a free grant of 160 acres of land. But it cannot afford to supply "religious privileges. That is your part. These men are doing "all they can, and so I appeal to the inherent love of fair play, "and deeply rooted sense of honour, which is part of the "Englishman's very being, and I say "Have I not a claim on "your support?" Help me to provide the men who shall go "alike to Indian and emigrant proclaiming the gospel of Him, "who was lifted up that he might draw all men unto Him. Let "us consider the position of the Indian population of these "regions. We so often listen to unfeeling remarks about "'survival of the fittest'" and are told "'that the native races "are dying out'" that our sympathies become blunted, and we "need reminding of the reply given by a chief, who said '"if we "are dying out, at least let us die Christians'."

This little book gives a glimpse at some of the mission work done among the water-ways of the diocese of Algoma, where the coast-line covers a thousand miles.

I, who was privileged to accompany the Bishop and his daughter and her friend for a ten days' trip on board the

"Evangeline," in order to visit the Islands with their interesting missions, and who enjoyed the hospitality of the missionary and his good wife at Sheguiandah; and saw how brightly and uncomplainingly the whole family put up with annoyances (such as the only cow being lost for two days in the bush, and the children being therefore without milk) can recommend the following pages, as giving an insight into the working of Indian missions, which may be fresh to many readers, and will I trust be considered worthy of perusal.

May I take the opportunity of once more pleading for men of devotion and ability, who possess sufficient private means for their own support, to devote themselves to the work of the Algoma Mission, especially the Indian branch thereof.

The Sheguiandah Indians are very kind and courteous in their demeanour. From the old woman who let me enter her wigwam, destitute and poverty-stricken as it was, to the "belle of the neighbourhood" who shared with me her Ojibway prayer book, and sang softly the hymns during the solemn services, where, with the exception of the Bishop and missionary, every person around me in that crowded church, was a native Christian, I received every attention and kindness.

It is sad to think of the poverty amongst these loyal people. The Government, in granting reserves to the Indians, or free grants to emigrants, retains the forest trees as its own property, and only permits their being cut down under certain conditions.

When I visited Birch Island (July 1890) I was struck with the beauty of its tall trees, throughout the neighbourhood. A year and a half later the Indians were so starved with cold and hunger that permission was given for them to cut the timber, and I am told that now the beauty of the spot is gone.

Years ago wild beasts abounded, and their flesh and skins provided the Indians with food and clothing. Now we have taught them to plant potatoes, but the following extract will show how few are the animals remaining.

"We are preparing for Christmas, and the Indians are getting "in provisions in the shape of a large bear that they have "killed—fat and big and good. They deserve the bear, having "been at work about a week to get him. They found his tracks "near a cave in the rocks, away back in the bush, and have been "hammering and blasting the rock, till they reached and "shot him. They skinned and then cut him up, and brought the "meat home. He will grace the Christmas feast. We shall "have service on Christmas Day. The Indians will decorate "the churches beautifully, and it will be a happy season for all. "We hope to have five or six Christmas trees in different parts "of my mission and then dispense the bounty of friends in "England and Canada."

That true Christmas joy may be the portion of many more bands of Ojibway Indians throughout the breadth of Algoma is the earnest desire of those who know this interesting people.

A. C. D.

AUTHOR'S PREFACE.

IN this little volume, it is proposed to give a brief and the Author fears a very imperfect account of some of the Church's work among Ojibway Indians and others domiciled, either upon, or in parts adjacent to, the Great Manitoulin Island in the vast missionary diocese of Algoma.

The Author commends it to all who are interested in the conversion of the heathen to the living God, or in the Church's mission to those whom business calls to reside in isolated places. He acknowledges his indebtedness to Miss DAY for her great assistance and access to her publications; to the pages of *The Algoma Missionary News;* to the writings of the late Ven. Archdeacon McMURRAY; to the Rev. Canon HURST, and to the Revs. F. FROST, J. H. McLEOD, and CHARLES PIERCEY, three of Algoma's zealous missionaries, for much valuable information, which has largely assisted him in compiling this work. He prays that its many shortcomings and imperfections may be forgiven.

CAMBRIDGE, *Easter*, 1895.

THE LORD'S PRAYER IN OJIBWAY.

Wayoosemegooyun kezhegoong ayahyun, Tahkecheahpeetandahgwud kedezhenekahzoowin; kedoogemahwewin; tahtuhgwisehnoomahgud; azhenundahwandahmun dahdoodaum oomah uhkeeng, debishkoo ewede ishpeming; Meezheshenaum noongoom kezheguk ka oonje pemahtezeyaung; Ahbwayanemeeshenaum kahmujjedoodahgooyunin azheahbwayanemungidwah egewh kahmujjedoodahweyungejig. Kagoo ezheweshehekaun kankuhgwatebanedewining; Ekooneshenaum atuh mujje-ezhewabezewening; Keen mahween kedebandaun oogemahwewin, kuhya dush ewh wahwezhanduhmoowin, kahgenig kuhya kahgenig. Amen.

CHAPTER I.

INTRODUCTION.

AMONG the letters opened by a clergyman at Cambridge immediately after chapel one morning in the May week of the present year (and May week, as everyone knows in Cambridge, commences the first or second Friday in June) were two of particular interest. One was from Mr. Frost, the clergyman in charge of Sheguiandah, and the second was from a critic who had just read the author's little book "Life in Algoma."

The former began, " I am writing a few words in reply to your type-written letter just received, although I have written often enough (God knows,) both to the different societies and to individuals in England, including an English lady whose name you will remember in connection with her visit to Manitoulin and the islands on the north shore. Still, I will write again, only with the stipulation that what I write you must take the trouble to read."

The other letter, after speaking of the book referred to, went on to regret that no sufficient mention had been made of the Indians resident in Algoma, and of the great work going on among them, and proceeded to suggest that a companion volume to " Life in

Algoma," giving some particulars of the work among the red men—one of whose chiefs welcomed the Bishop as " The Great Black Coat " sent to teach them the religion of " Their great Mother, the Queen "—would not only be interesting, but of value also.

Before the day was out a third letter came to hand, this time from a lady. She regretted that in " Life in Algoma " more had not been said about lumbermen, and that no account had been given of corduroy and other rough roads. Well, all these things were omitted in that book because they did not exist to any great extent in the part of the diocese upon which the book treated. The lumber interest was on a much smaller scale than in other parts; there were no Indians at all; and corduroy roads were of the shortest length and had almost entirely been superseded by others.

The three letters, arriving the same day at the college residence of the clergyman, caused him to determine to follow the advice given; and, if possible, to give his readers some information about the Indians of the Manitoulin Island, and those employed in the great lumber interest located there. This island is situated in lake Huron, and is over one hundred miles in length. There are innumerable bays and creeks and mouths of rivers both on the shores of the island and on the shore of the mainland opposite. Upon the island, and on the mainland in its immediate vicinity, are several English and Indian

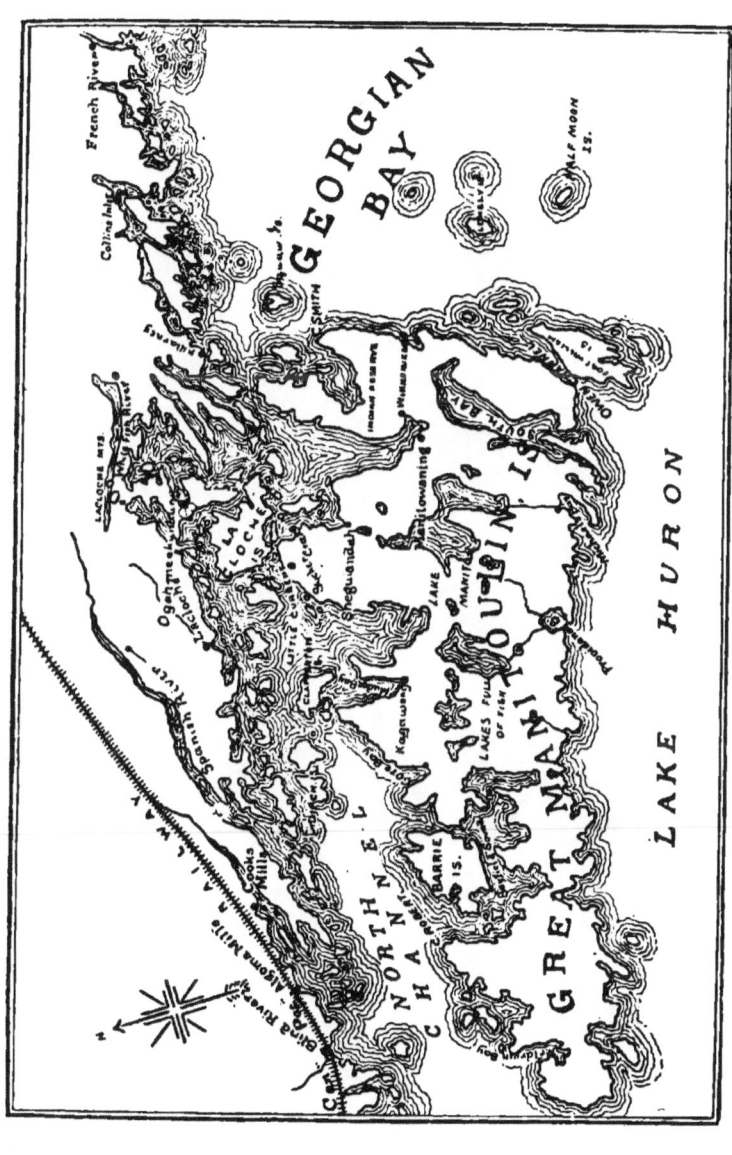

MAP OF THE MANITOULIN ISLAND

[To face p. 16.

villages, besides many lumber camps and other places to which, during the winter, the missionaries make periodical trips, such as McDonald's Camp, Beaverstone, Bad River, Beaver Meadow, Cromline Point, and others.

There are three important missions in the Manitoulin Island—Gore Bay, Manitowaning, and Sheguiandah. That of Manitowaning is, I believe, the original one of the Red Indians, who, thirty years ago, had no organised mission or resident clergyman, the christian Indians being represented by individuals who at Walpole Island or elsewhere had come under the teaching of the Church of England. Of late Manitowaning, being without its own clergyman, has been visited occasionally by the Rev. F. Frost, whose mission of Sheguiandah, distant sixteen miles from Manitowaning and including the adjacent country for a radius of fifty miles, will be treated of in the following pages.

At Sheguiandah are two villages about two miles apart, the first being inhabited (with the exception of the missionary and his family) by Ojibway Indians to whom chief Manitowahsing gives an example of sterling worth and christian living. The second by English settlers, who, as well as the Indians, have their church, in which services are regularly held each Sunday.

Little Current is the principal place on the eastern side of the island, and is touched by the steamships of the Great Northern Transit Company. Sucker Creek, distant about four miles from Little Current, has a schoolhouse for its Indian population, and occasional services are held in it.

Aundagwahmenekauning, situated on lovely Birch Island, sixteen miles from Little Current, has an Indian congregation of about fifty souls. Unfortunately the whole band now numbers less than one hundred persons, the population having decreased of late years.

On the mainland opposite Sheguiandah, and some twenty miles off, there is a peninsula; situated thereon is an Indian village named Ogahmeekunaung, which is visited, as well as the English Mission Stations of Killarney and Collin's Inlet, by this indefatigable Missionary.

Further west, still on the mainland, he goes to White Fish River and Spanish River. This last village is difficult of approach during the summer season on account of the number of portages—those places where, in rivers largely used for navigation, we should find locks. Notwithstanding all possible assistance being given to him by the Indians, the transportation of tent, bedding and other requirements, including food, becomes very trying.

The Rev. J. H. McLeod has the headquarters of his Mission at Gore Bay; Burpee, Kagawong, and Meldrum Bay being out-stations under his charge.

The chief resources of the district are undoubtedly

its minerals, its forests, and its fisheries. Squaw Island at the southern end of the Great Manitoulin Island, is perhaps one of the chief fishing stations of the inland sea in which it is situated; while the Great Island itself abounds in minerals, amongst others being a valuable limestone. This limestone is at present being used in the construction of the locks upon the large ship canal at Sault Sainte Marie, the See-town of the Diocese. We are told by Mr. Alan Sullivan, in his excellent article upon Algoma, that the tonnage passing through this canal in seven months exceeds that of the Suez Canal for a whole year.

Farming is gradually being carried on to a larger extent, and upon the Island there are districts containing large areas of some of the finest farming land in the country. Particularly is this true of some thousands of acres near Gore Bay. Dairy farming is also an increasing industry, and a large and growing trade is now carried on in butter for the Toronto Market. Another point which is worthy of notice is the steady improvement of the Indian as an agriculturist.

The roads in the district are of very inferior quality, and cause travelling to be a matter of difficulty during spring and autumn when they are at their worst. In the summer it is made easier on account of the open waters of the lakes and rivers; but even then places that are distant from the shore are difficult of access, for one can scarcely put a horse and buggy into a canoe or row-boat, and without such aid there is much loss of time and strength. Even when it is available the position of affairs is not much better, for the thick bush keeps the so-called roads very wet, and, if the road happen to be corduroy, the rough trunks are often alternated with mud-holes, in which there is danger of the horse being engulfed, only to be rescued with care and labour.

Winter changes all this, and is indeed the time *par excellence* for the missionary, the Indian, and the settler. Then, with the lanes and rivers converted into hard roads, they can drive from place to place without delay and with less fatigue, to say nothing of its being pleasanter to glide over the snow than to bump along over bush roads. But winter has its own difficulties; the ice and snow are not always in good condition. The former sometimes gives way, and both horse and driver are swallowed up in the depth below; and snowstorms come, often forming deep and impassable drifts. The scenery as a whole is usually very beautiful, particularly in the autumn and winter; but there are times when it is extremely dreary. But, after all, the autumn or "Indian summer" is perfect both as to temperature by night or day, and also as to the beauty of the forest scenery.

CHAPTER II.

Early Days.

No account of the work among Ojibway Indians could well be written without some reference to the late Archdeacon McMurray, who was the first missionary sent to them. In August, 1832, he was sent for by the Lieutenant Governor of Upper Canada, Sir John Colborne, and informed that his excellency had decided to establish a series of missions amongst the Ojibway Indians. Acting in concert with the "Society for Converting and Civilising the Indians," he had singled out Mr. McMurray—who was then a candidate for holy orders—for this important work. His head-quarters were to be at Sault Ste Marie. Never having heard of such a place, he naturally asked where it was; but neither his excellency nor the surveyor general could point out the place, as no survey of that distant region had then been made.

It was then suggested that he should go to Buffalo and Detroit and if possible acquire the necessary information. It was a bold step for one so young and inexperienced, yet he accepted the offer, and informed his excellency that if the requisite credentials were prepared he would leave for the " terra incognita." He started in September, and after a long and hazardous voyage, partly by steamer, schooner and canoe, he reached his future home just one month later. This distance can now be accomplished in seventy-six hours.

His first object was to procure a shelter, for the whole country was one dense forest. By the kindness of the governor of the Hudson Bay Company, lodgings for the winter were given him in the house of the Company's agents. He lost no time in summoning the Indians to meet him in council, to lay before them the object of his mission. He told them that Church and Government desired their conversion and civilisation. The old chief, Shingwahcase, a most fluent and able speaker, presented him with the pipe of peace, and addressed him as follows:—

"We desire first to know whether you can give us any assurance that you have been sent by our Great Father at York" (now Toronto). Mr. McMurray at once produced his credentials, having the seal of the province attached. The chief compared them with his own medal and was satisfied that he was duly accredited. Having previously learnt that the Indians were given to intoxication, Mr. McMurray took this opportunity of reproving them. The reply of the chief was characteristic, but must have come as a great reproof to the young missionary. "My fathers never knew how to cultivate the land; my fathers never knew how to build mills; my fathers never knew how to extract the devil's broth out of the grain. You make it and bring it to us, and you blame us for drinking it."

The result of this council was the establishment of services, which were held in Mr. McMurray's room, there being no other available place. He was not yet ordained, so the next step was to learn the whereabouts of the only Bishop in Canada at that time— the saintly Bishop Stewart. As there was no regular mail communication at Sault Sainte Marie from November to May, he went to York hoping to find the Bishop there. But in this he was disappointed, and it was not before he had travelled to Kingston and Montreal—in all a distance of 1,500 miles—that he found the Bishop at St. Armand's. Here he was ordained, August 11th, 1833. He lost no time in returning to his mission, and a month later he reached Sault Sainte Marie.

An incident that occurred about this time will serve to show the awakening of the Indians' hearts. The chief's youngest son was very ill, and Mr. McMurray had been reading to the invalid and praying for his recovery. Shingwahcase listened very attentively, and at length exclaimed, "Why should not I also offer up prayer to the Great Spirit on behalf of my son?" Then he fell on his knees, and poured out his soul in eloquent and touching words. The missionary was beginning to reap the fruit of his labours, the Indians one by one abandoned their superstitions, and were willing to open their ears to the gospel message.

The Lieutenant Governor, having heard of his success, suggested that Mr. McMurray should bring a few of the Indians to York. He was anxious to converse with them, and doubtless thought that a visit to the town might encourage their efforts at civilisation. So Shingwahcase and six others journeyed to York. That they might not be tempted to drink the "devil's broth" the thoughtful missionary lodged them in a dense grove of pines on the spot where the church of Holy Trinity now stands. They were soon summoned to an interview with the Lieutenant Governor and received much kind and useful advice. His excellency also gave the chief a flag which he was to hoist over his wigwam every Sunday.

During the administration of Sir John Colborne the work among the Indians advanced very satisfactorily, but under his successor there was a cessation of the support which the Government had before given. Mr. McMurray resigned, and the Indians were left to make what advance they could without his assistance. For twelve years they did what they could. Sunday by Sunday the old chief raised his flag over his wigwam to assemble his people. So they observed the day that is dedicated to the service of that Saviour whom they were beginning to know and love. They used the prayers they had been taught to say, they repeated portions of Scripture that their memory retained, and sang some hymns they had learnt from the missionary. Thus the Ojibway Indians showed their desire to profit by the instructions they received. Their faith and patience were at length rewarded by the late Dr. O'Meara being appointed to the Mission, whose devoted services they afterwards much appreciated.

The following incident will show that they were also anxious to further the spread of the Gospel. A missionary was once telling them that they owed much to the kindness of English people who gave money in support of the Missions, and how that they also had a duty towards those Indians who had not yet heard the "glad tidings." The chief acknowledged the truth of this "but" he said, turning to the Missionary, "our father here knows that we Indians have not yellow money (gold), nor white money (silver), nor even red money (copper). But I will tell you what we ca   o. In a few weeks we shall all be leaving   of ours and going out into the sugar bush.   that the earliest produce of the tapped   is always the fairest and best of the   us put by some of this and bring it to   , and he will sell it to the trader and   to the Society to be used for sending   the Gospel to parts which are still

Two months after an old Indian woman arrived at the Missionary's house carrying a large basket of sugar, which she said was the first-fruits of her. sugar harvest. She requested that it might be put into the Missionary barrel for her. One after another, the Indians brought similar contributions for the same purpose, so that two barrels of the fairest and best sugar were available for sale. Every pound of this represented self-denial on the part of those who had given, and who would have to go without some comfort which the sugar would have procured.

CHAPTER III.

SHEGUIANDAH.

SHEGUIANDAH consists of two villages, the Indian village, and the white. The population of the former is entirely Indian, and all are members of the Church. On Sunday morning a service is held at nine o'clock, which they attend in good numbers, and with evident satisfaction. The services are rendered entirely in Ojibway, having been translated into that tongue by Dr. O'Meara, with the help of one of the natives. The New Testament and part of the Old were also translated by the same clergyman. Several week-day gatherings are held both in the Church and school-house. On Sunday afternoons the Missionary's wife conducts the Sunday School, with the assistance of an Indian teacher who also, when the Missionary is absent, takes the evening service.

At White Village there is a pretty little church on the hill where there is a service in English at 11 a.m. on Sunday, and at other times during the week. Here too the people attend well, but the congregation is small and scattered, and many who would come are often prevented by the terrible state of the roads in bad weather.

Much useful work was accomplished by Mr. Frost

the clergyman in charge of the Mission, during the winter months, for then travelling is made easy by the frozen state of the snow and lakes. Several visits to distant stations were made. In one of his tours he visited La Cloche, Spanish River and Moncason, at which places he held services, and was occasionally called upon to baptize children. On his return journey he called at Webbwood, and then proceeded to a shanty at a distance of twelve miles, on the way visiting some cabins in the bush. Here a very rough congregation assembled, but they were most attentive, and several helped on the Church's work by giving donations.

Returning to Webbwood next day, he was asked by several men to hold a service. With the object of finding out the wishes of the population he made several calls. He discovered a few Church people and many who professed other religions, and some who professed none at all. However, a service was held in the house of a storekeeper who had offered it for the purpose, and a hearty one it proved to be and was much enjoyed by a large congregation. Next day, which was Saturday, the Missionary started to return home. He had a distance of nearly fifty miles to travel before nightfall, and this he was able to accomplish owing to an early start and good roads. The following day he took the usual services at Sheguiandah, and during the week he went to Gore Bay; here he met with an English family who had

SHEGUINANDAH CHURCH

SHEGUIANDAH.   31

come from a village near his own home in England.
We can easily imagine how much pleasure it must
have afforded them to speak of the old days spent in
their native land. But Mr. Frost was not idle at
Gore Bay, for he held two services, and celebrated
the Holy Communion at St. Paul's Church, at which
the offertory amounted to ten dollars.

This, then, was some of his winter's work, which
was rendered impossible in the spring owing to the
breaking up of the ice. During this season the
missionary was obliged to confine his work to the
limits of Manitoulin Island. Even here the roads
were at times a great hindrance to his getting
about. However, many gatherings were held at
Sheguiandah and also at Sucker Creek, where on
Monday evenings the younger members of the
population would assemble to receive instruction in
the prayer book. But at length the ice disappeared
from the rivers and lakes, and it was again possible to make use of navigation. Gore Bay was
again visited, this time by steamboat.

Mr. Frost was the possessor of a little sailing boat,
which had been presented to him by the children of
Grace Church Sunday School, Toronto. In this boat
he now took a trip, having engaged the services of an
Indian to assist in its management. First they sailed
to La Cloche, where the boat was left, and a birch-
bark canoe procured, which could easily be carried
over the portages. Thus they reached a village near

the river, where it was found that the Indians had been making preparations for building a church, which was to be commenced as soon as they had planted their gardens. White-fish river was next visited. The Indians here conferred with the missionary about building a church and schoolhouse. The material for the latter building had been promised by the Indian department of the Canadian Government.

Another trip taken by Mr. Frost about this time was to Collin's Inlet, the journey being made by steamboat and tug. At the inlet he borrowed a skiff and rowed down to Beaverstone. Collin's Inlet is only a small village. In the middle is a mill, round which the wooden cottages are clustered; on the rocks, a little to one side of the village, stands the schoolhouse, where services are held. In the winter the villagers are mostly employed in the woods getting out pine logs which are cut up at the mill during the summer. Beaverstone is situated on the banks of a small river about twenty-five miles from Killarney. It is a wood depôt, and the chief employment is cutting pulp wood which is much used in the manufacture of paper, pails, and many other articles.

At the mouth of the river the missionary found some of his parishioners, and with these he had lunch in the open air. The "menu" included pork, bread and rice pudding. The luncheon was followed by a short address, and in the evening a service was held at a depôt twelve miles distant. This depôt had to be reached by a very rough road that was carried over ravines by bridges that often consisted of a tree laid across, Some people, whom Mr. Frost wished to visit, lived on the other side of the river; but he was a little afraid of crossing the river on floating logs, so they came over to him. Several men returned with him to Collin's Inlet, and as a large number were working at the mill, he determined to hold a service. But it was a busy evening with the men, and only a few attended. As the tug left next morning this was their last opportunity of hearing the missionary for the present, a circumstance which was not only regretted by the clergyman, but, also by many of the people, some of whom had hoped he would be able to stay a day or two longer with them.

   Carpe diem, quam minimum
  Credula postero. HOR. CARM. i., 11.

CHAPTER IV.

Christmas among the Indians.

LATE in the autumn the "Evangeline," the Bishop's Mission Steamer, arrived at Sheguiandah with his Lordship on board. The Bishop and Mr. Frost together visited an Indian village, situated about twelve miles from the mouth of Spanish River; this village is itself known by the name of Spanish River. Communication between it and Sheguiandah —from which it is distant about thirty miles—is by water in summer and across ice in winter. Nearly all the Indians are now Christians, and to Mr. Frost is due the credit of having converted them from heathenism. During the summer they had built a neat little church of wood, and a schoolhouse, the materials having been given to them, and the Indians giving their labour.

The Bishop now came to open the Church, and was much pleased with the building, congratulating the Indians on their perseverance. He preached on the subject, "Christ the Good Shepherd," and held the Service of Confirmation. There is now at Spanish River a school teacher who also acts as catechist, receiving his instructions from the Missionary. That same evening the Bishop and Mr.

Frost steamed down the river to the mill and held a service in the schoolhouse, the congregation consisting largely of men employed at the mill.

Next day they intended to visit White Fish River and then go on to Collin's Inlet. The weather was far too stormy and rough to allow of this. They therefore sailed down the lake as far as Killarney, and there spent the night. Here fishing forms the chief occupation of the inhabitants, who are for the most part half-breeds; a large number of the people are Roman Catholics, but there are some members of the Church of England, and these value very highly the occasional services that are held there by the Missionary.

Soon after the Bishop's departure from the Sheguiandah Mission, the frost began to have its wonted effect upon the water. The Indians thought that each day would be the last of the summer season, and that grim winter would return and lock all in its iron grasp, converting the water-ways into plains of ice, over which once more they would travel upon snowshoes, with their teams of dogs by their side, drawing their belongings from one place to another, as they camped about or brought in articles from a distance. November came, and with it the frozen seas; and the Great Manitoulin, and other Islands, all became united to the mainland by excellent roads of ice.

Then, a few weeks later, the great festival for

which all our children long and make so thoroughly their own, returned. Let us see how the Indian Christians in Algoma spend their Christmas. At Sheguiandah the pretty little church was nicely decorated, and on Christmas Eve a large congregation of Indians gathered to worship the Saviour, Whose birth is commemorated so joyfully by all Christians at this happy season. With great spirit did the Indians in their own tongue sing the Christmas Hymn "Hark! the Herald Angels sing," and they entered into the other parts of the service with evident interest and enjoyment. The sermon was on the "angels' message to the shepherds" and was preached in Ojibway by Mr. Frost; then on Christmas morning a large number received the Holy Communion in obedience to Christ's command, and so many came to the nine o'clock ervice that the church was not large enough to admit all. Some had come from a great distance, and over ice which had made their travelling both difficult and dangerous. Mr. Frost chose as the text for his sermon the words, "and will God in very deed dwell with man on the earth?" Then, at the close of the service there was much hearty handshaking between the clergyman and his congregation, and a great many kind Christmas wishes were exchanged.

The next evening the chief gave an entertainment to the village children, consisting of a Christmas tree

It was laden with candles and other small articles, chiefly made by the members of his own family. Mr. Frost was presented with a gorgeous hanging basket, and some grass work was given to Mrs. Frost. When all the treasures on the tree had been distributed, two Indian youths conducted an exhibition which proved very successful and a source of great amusement to the young people.

A few days later the usual Christmas-tree entertainment was given in the schoolhouse, when many useful articles of clothing, blankets and quilts (the gift of the Women's Auxiliary, a well-known Church of England Society having branches in nearly every Canadian parish), were distributed to those Indians who were most in need of such help, and to whom, consequently, they were most acceptable. One of the Indians requested the Missionary to thank the givers of these useful presents. Eighty-five Indians were present, and at the close of the evening all joined in singing "God save the Queen."

At another Indian village, on the Manitoulin Island, the church was also beautifully decorated: The walls were spotlessly white, having recently been whitewashed, so that the decorations, which consisted mostly of dark evergreens, stood out very clearly. After the service here on Christmas Day, Mr. Frost was invited to be present at a public Indian feast, but he was unable to accept their hospitality. On New Year's Eve the village was enlivened by a social function, at which a Christmas tree formed a great attraction. Those people who think that the Indians never laugh should have been present on this occasion, for their hearty laughter and beaming faces must have caused them to change their opinion on the subject. As at Sheguiandah, a arge quantity of clothing was distributed amongst the Indians. Many orphan children were sent home with sufficient to clothe them from head to foot.

Several of these articles came from England, and were the handiwork of a band of workers, who for many years have cheerfully worked hand in hand with a lady residing in Sussex. Some of these workers are of the poorest, yet they regularly, with unfailing energy, work upon the articles supplied to them for the use of their less favoured brethren; whose faces may not be so fair as their own, yet whose hearts are as pure. Only those who have witnessed the pleasure the work gives to the ready and willing helpers, can realise anything of the joy depicted upon their faces when speaking of the work they have been enabled to do; done, not for the lady whom many both in town and country have risen up to call blessed, but done for that Saviour who gave His life for the red man as much as for us.

CHAPTER V.

BAD TRAVELLING.

Snow, snow everywhere; on trees, land and water. Fences and stumps had disappeared; all was one plain of spotless snow, as soft and as white as swansdown. The very trees appeared as in bridal attire, and the old black pines, killed by the recent forest fires, stood out like gaunt spectres. One might perhaps think that nothing—save the beautiful autumnal tints of the ever-varying foliage—could look more gloriously beautiful than the scene before us on this early winter's day; and when the snow clouds have cleared away and the incomparable Canadian sun bursts out from behind the driving curack, tinging with gold the surface of the snow, and infusing into the scene a flush of life and hope, the spectator feels that God has indeed reserved much of the beauty and grandeur of creation for Canada's distant shores. But although the scene was a beautiful one, this same snow—newly fallen and treacherous, —rendered travelling a matter of difficulty and danger. wor until the sun has caused it to "pack" it is as loose as the desert sand, and, what is worse, neither man nor horse can travel over it without sinking at every step to the solid surface beneath.

But let the sun shine on it for a few hours, and the nightly frosts do their work, and then both man and beast can travel without danger of breaking the upper crust. This usually happens within a few hours of a heavy fall, but woe to those who must journey either during a storm of blinding snow or before it has become thus hardened.

Sometimes, again, the ice of the rivers continues in an unsafe condition for weeks on account of the frequent rise and fall of water. It was in consequence of the unsafe condition of the ice, that the missionary was unable to undertake any extended journey from his home during the early part of the year. Later on, finding that a crossing had been made to the north shore of lake Huron, he made preparations to go there, although the ice was far from safe. Part of the distance could be traversed on land, but when the ice was reached, Mr. Frost found there was but a single track to guide him across the frozen expanse. However, he knew the general direction which he ought to take; consequently he was not much troubled about the slight and imperfect indications of the road. Throughout the travelling was bad, and especially so in places where the crust of the snow was not sufficiently strong to bear the weight of his horse. Beneath this crust was water which was sometimes of such a depth that he had misgivings as to whether there was any ice at all below the water. This frequent breaking of the upper crust of the snow naturally hindered his progress, but in some places he was able to advance at a fair pace, especially when the way led by the shores of an island, where the ice was almost glare, or free from snow. Before nightfall he fortunately reached an Indian settlement.

He held a service in the chief's house, which served for a church. It had recently been repaired and enlarged, and in it Mr. Frost was made very comfortable during his stay in the settlement. A large congregation of Indians assembled for the service, and at the close a council was held at which the desirability of building a church was discussed. Here, too, a Christmas tree formed part of the proceedings, and many warm garments were given to the children and old people. These garments had been given by a branch of the Women's Auxiliary.

The next day a snowstorm came on; yet the energetic missionary pursued his journey, and arrived without mishap at another Indian village, situated on the banks of a river. It was pleasant to observe that the Indians had improved their dwellings since his last visit and that two new and substantially built log houses had been erected. He selected the largest house in the place and there held a service. Notwithstanding the fact that a large number of Indians were absent from the village at work in the lumber shanties, a very good congregation met together. Mr. Frost addressed them, taking the Epiphany as his subject.

In the afternoon he returned through the bush, crossing some picturesque lakes and passing through some very dense thickets where constant care was required lest the sleigh should catch against the trees and be overturned. Thick and fast fell the snow, crashing down from the towering pine trees, blinding the driver and impeding his horse, but just before nightfall he happily reached a lumber shanty; and as it was so late and it would be impossible to reach home, he gladly accepted the men's invitation to stay with them that night; especially as it afforded him an opportunity of addressing them. As there was still a little daylight left he watched the men loading logs, and helped to saw some. He was most kindly treated, and his horse was given the best stall in the stable and an abundant supply of hay and oats.

When the horses had been fed, the men themselves sat down to supper, a considerable quantity of wholesome provisions being provided. After supper the missionary waited for an opportunity to address them, but all set about some employment such as sewing on buttons or mending whips, or talking over the day's events. However, the foreman informed him that as soon as the men had finished their various little occupations there would be a good opportunity for speaking, as all would then be quiet in the camp. At length the missionary began his address, which

A LOAD OF LOGS.

was listened to with respectful attention ; then they sang and prayed, and some donations were given towards the mission. One young man, a member of the Church of England, invited Mr. Frost to share his bunk. This bunk was close to the stove in which a roaring fire was burning and the heat was so intense that it was impossible to sleep. Then again, in the sleeping apartments of a lumber camp there is always a frowsy smell that is very unpleasant.

However, the missionary and his companion conversed together till long after the rest of the camp were asleep, and after a while the heat of the stove became less intense, so that sleep for them also became possible. Long before daybreak the camp was astir ; the teamsters were out feeding their horses, and at five o'clock breakfast was ready. After this Mr. Frost asked the foreman if he might read a chapter from the Bible to the men. He was readily granted permission to do so. Then he was presented with a new cross-cut saw, an axe, a pair of warm oversocks, and some oats for his horse, and so in the early morning they parted and went to their different work; the men to their logs, the missionary to Sheguiandah..

CHAPTER VI.

INDIAN SUPERSTITIONS.

EARLY in the year the missionary set out on a long journey to visit a young Indian who was dying. His destination lay on the banks of a river, and when he had travelled for nearly the whole day he was met by an Indian boy. This boy told him he was still ten miles distant from the village, and that his journey was useless, as the Indian had died on the previous day, and had been buried that morning. Great was the disappointment felt by Mr. Frost that his long and fatiguing journey was taken to no purpose, and that death had been before him.

However, on learning that a large number of friends and relations were still at the house so lately visited by the Great Destroyer, he determined to press on. It was already getting late, but he had a guide to lead him over that long, dreary river, with its monotonous banks covered with rocks and woods. Night came on before half the distance had been traversed. The river widened into a sort of lagoon; the rocky shores were left, and there was nothing to be seen but an expanse of snow, with here and there a tree stretching out its bare limbs. These trees had been washed down by the current during the floods of spring, and were now fast held by the ice.

Just before midnight, Mr. Frost and his guide reached the cabin, which was found to be full of Indians; men and women sitting about on the floor. The parents greatly regretted that the boy had been buried before the missionary's arrival, for no "black coat" had been present to pray when the body was lowered into the grave. They welcomed him joyfully and were glad he had come to speak to them about religion. First they attended to his earthly wants, giving him supper, which consisted of trout and potatoes. A service followed at which they all sang in their own tongue the hymn "Jesu, lover of my soul," and the missionary explained the mysteries and glories of the resurrection from the dead.

In a small room, partitioned off from the main cabin, the missionary sought the repose and sleep which he so sadly needed after his trying day's work. Sleep did not come very readily, for the Indians continued in the cabin, and the sound of their voices in conversation reached him. When at length he did sleep, it was only for a short time. Suddenly he was awakened by shouting and stamping of feet; a noise as of tables and chairs overturning, a rushing from the cabin, a yelling and whooping. Then all was still; the whole party he could hear had left the cabin and were rushing about in the open air. He thought that perhaps some moose or cariboo were coming down the river, or that a herd of deer was passing, or perhaps even a pack of wolves; and that the Indians had gone forth in a body to attack the invaders.

To be suddenly awakened from sleep by a loud and unintelligible noise is by no means agreeable; and being thus left alone in a strange place, it is not to be wondered at that Mr. Frost felt very alarmed. He crept out of bed; then he ventured into the cabin and looked out from the door. Standing near he observed an old woman, and enquired of her the cause of all the commotion. She replied that a large owl had come after the chickens, and the Indians were frightening it off. With some misgivings and not at all inclined to believe that the woman had told him the true cause of the disturbance, the missionary returned to his bed. In the morning the Indians would give no explanation of their extraordinary conduct of the previous evening, so Mr. Frost, having read the morning prayers, began his homeward journey still ignorant of the cause and nature of the nocturnal disturbance.

Not long after he was spending the night at another Indian village. His host, a young and intelligent Indian, in the course of conversation, mentioned that there had been a funeral in the neighbourhood a day or so before. The missionary then gave an account of the noises he had heard at the other village, and the old woman's story of an owl. The young man cleared up the mystery by the following explanation: "The Indians believe that within three days of the death and burial of anyone, the Evil Spirit comes to the grave in the form of an owl. He shoots out fire from his beak, he stands on the grave and the coffin comes up. Then he takes out the heart of the dead man, and carries it away. What the Indian has to do is to frighten away the owl before he can do any mischief to the dead."

Here then was the clue to the Indians' strange conduct that night in the cabin on the banks of the river. But did they really see an owl, or was their imagination heightened by superstitious belief? These Indians were not altogether ignorant, and the fact of their silence, and the story of the owl and the chickens told by the old woman, seem to show that they knew their superstitious customs could not meet with approval from the missionary. Moreover, the parents of the boy who had died used to read their Bible and Prayer Book every day, and were firm believers in the Christian religion. Evidently some belief in the old heathen fable still clung to them and made them disinclined to abandon their superstitious practices entirely.

Amongst the Indians there is also a very strong belief in witchcraft. Mr. Frost was once asked to reprove a man who was accused of practising "vile and devilish arts." He found it a hard matter trying to make the Indians believe that no one by arts of magic had power to do them any harm. Still they persisted that the sorcerers made hieroglyphics on the barks of trees near their houses which were the cause of illness to the inmates. Only by time and patient instruction can superstition be overcome. Sometimes the missionaries find intelligent and well-instructed Indians holding belief in such absurd and silly superstitions that it is a trying matter to be patient with them.

One afternoon Mr. Frost had been preaching upon belief in fables. After the service a young Indian stood up in the congregation and said: " I have to say that I don't believe in these old Indian fables; yet I think to myself, I wonder if they are not true. Were all our forefathers deceived? But I know that this nonsense is not God's truth. If we are Christians we must believe only in Christ. Some people think that whiskey is the ruin of the Indian ; but it is not whiskey, it is witchcraft."

The Indians used to make offerings of corn and sugar and tobacco to the dead. In the case of a child these offerings consisted of candies, berries and toys. The missionary endeavours to teach them that the life of the soul in the next world is not as the life of the body in this. Though they read in holy scripture of eating and drinking in heaven, they must understand it to refer to spiritual enjoyment. Neither dead bodies or living souls have any need of their offerings.

When shall the untutored heathen tribes,
A dark bewildered race,
Sit down at our Immanuel's feet,
And learn and feel his grace ?

Smile, Lord, on each divine attempt
To spread the gospel's rays :
And rear on sin's demolished throne
The temples of thy praise.
Kemble.

CHAPTER VII.

An Ice Accident.

During March Mr. Frost was actively engaged in his work at Beaverstone, Gromline Point, Collin's Inlet and other places in the neighbourhood. He held a service at Killarney, which the whole population of the place attended. On the following day he again held a service at a place about twenty miles distant, which he had last visited about six months before. During that period there had been no services, but the children had attended the Sunday School with great regularity. Mr. Frost remained here over Sunday, and both the morning and evening services were well attended. On leaving this place he travelled through the bush in a northerly direction, and visited a shanty in the neighbourhood of Lake Penage. Here his congregation consisted of twenty-three persons of several different nationalities. All were glad to see him, and to have an opportunity of joining in the service. One young man had recently left his home in England, and it was a pleasure to the missionary to converse with one whose memories of that country were so fresh. The next day he went to a shanty where the majority of the inmates were Frenchmen. Although they doubtless failed to understand much of the service, they listened very attentively, and, it is to be hoped, received benefit from it.

After leaving this shanty Mr. Frost met with an accident ; yet he can say with David " I was in trouble and He helped me." A heavy fall of snow the previous night had caused him to be longer than usual on the road. Towards noon he had reached the river and was driving through a channel between rocks, when his horse suddenly dropped through the ice. No one was at hand to help him in his trouble, so unaided he set about rescuing the unfortunate horse. The first thing to be done was to free it of the sleigh ; in many places the missionary had to cut the harness, being unable to unfasten it. Then he fastened the reins round the animal's neck and pulled with all his strength. The poor creature, numbed with the cold, seemed both unable and unwilling to help itself. But at length it began to struggle, and then Mr Frost succeeded in getting the fore feet on to the ice, and by dragging it on to its side, finally landed it on firm ice. Then he led it back, leaving the sleigh and part of the harness at the scene of the mishap.

But before he had reached the shore, the ice again gave way. This time he was almost inclined to abandon the horse, being unable to extricate its legs from a crack in the ice. However, after many useless attempts he succeeded, and in the course of an hour it was lodged in a comfortable stable, much wounded, and unfit to work for some time. So Mr. Frost was compelled to pursue his journey on foot, with his dog drawing his rugs, overcoat and satchel.

Nor was Mr. Frost the only one who met with an accident on the ice at this time. The day proved to be a fatal one to a team of horses working at another river. Here the teams had for days been at work hauling logs and placing them upon the ice, and each day some thirty to forty loads had been safely drawn over a lumber road, which for two or three miles ran across a small lake. The last load for the day had been safely deposited, and the teams were on their way back to the camp for the night.

The last team, having nothing behind it but the sleigh, empty, save that the driver was as usual riding thereon, had reached to within three or four times its own length of the shore, when the ice, which before had safely carried ton upon ton, now suddenly gave way, and both horses and driver were without warning immersed. The drivers of the other teams, hearing their comrade's cry for help, at once came to his assistance. Nothing could been seen of the horses beyond their heads, and one of them seemed quite unable to move. The weight of the sleigh was doubtless keeping the horses down, and probably the poor animals' legs had become entangled in the chains and harness.

Every means was used to help the poor creatures,

but without avail; the ice was so unsafe around them, that they were reached only with difficulty and great danger. Not even the whole of the chains from the other teams served to make a sufficiently long cable to reach from the unfortunate team to a spot were a footing for the other horses could be obtained. Thus they were unable to put a chain round the necks of the horses that were immersed, and pull them out by main force. The water was terribly cold, and in half-an-hour death had released the poor animals from their sufferings. The driver himself (who was the owner of the horses) had a very narrow escape from drowning, and his exposure caused him a severe illness. These horses were the whole of the poor fellow's capital, the result of many years of hard work and self-denial.

Thus Mr. Frost proceeded on his journey, and completed his tour on foot. On the evening following the accident to his horse, he arrived in the neighbourhood of the Beaverstone River. At noon next day he addressed a few persons at the depôt, and in the evening held a service in the neighbourhood of Bad River. During the day he walked a distance of twelve miles, through the bush and on the river. He next went to see the Indians at Point Gromline and held a service at a very clean and respectable Indian house. At this place he baptised the widow of a former chief, who was known by the name of Ahmiticoegors. She had been a Pagan all her life, and had recently been converted to Christianity. Her brother has been a christian for many years, and at his house there are family prayers regularly both morning and evening.

Mr. Frost visited all the Indians at Point Gromline, and in the evening returned to the depôt. The following day was Sunday, and a large congregation attended the morning service, many Indians being present. There was a second service for the Indians in the afternoon, at the close of which the missionary returned to the place where he had left his horse. He found it somewhat better, so determined in the morning to start on his journey to Sheguiandah. After travelling only a few miles, it was evident that the horse could go no further. Mr. Frost was accordingly compelled to give it a few days' rest; after which he proceeded to Killarney, going at the rate of about two miles an hour. At Killarney he stayed the night and next day reached his home without further accident.

THE "EVANGELINE."

E

CHAPTER VIII.

"The Evangeline."

IT is not intended to give a history or lengthy account of the "Evangeline," but in passing it may be mentioned that formerly she was used as a pleasure yacht, and owned by H.R.H. the Prince of Wales. Doubtless in those days she was a bright and elegant vessel fitted and equipped in a manner worthy of her royal owner, and would be the object of many an admiring glance when riding at anchor off Cowes. At this time she was called the "Zenobia," and when offered for sale was purchased by the English supporters of the diocese of Algoma for the use of the Bishop.

And here we fancy some one saying: "What a luxury." But was it a luxury? Was it not rather necessity that prompted the purchase? In the vast diocese of Algoma there are dwellers who can only be reached by some such means as a private vessel for the Bishop. People who live in isolated fishing stations and lighthouses; Indian villages and lumber camps; many places that in those days were connected by no ordinary line of steamers, or other means of transit, and many places that have still no regular communication with the more important towns.

Manitoulin Island alone has a very extensive coast-line, much indented, and is surrounded by an enormous number of small islands. Then, again, scattered about at various points on the shores of the great lakes or inland seas, are groups of men far removed from religious privileges. There are the tribes of Ojibway Indians, diminished greatly in number it is true, but still the representatives of those who in former times were the rightful owners of the land, and who now have allotted to them by Government certain districts called reserves. All these could not be regularly visited by their episcopal head, were he not provided with some suitable vessel. And then as to luxury: well let us see. Fare: ordinarily, canned meat and boiled potatoes, varied occasionally by a roast joint brought on board from home, before weighing anchor. Bed: a hair cushion, as soft and yielding as the cabin floor. Weather: what Providence sends; now calm and sunshine, and again rain, hail and wind, with nothing to shelter the episcopal pilot—who never leaves the wheel—save an ample tarpaulin. Such is the luxurious life on board the "Evangeline." The Bishop never complains; should others?

But to return to the "Zenobia." After her purchase she was shipped from Liverpool and ten years ago safely reached the diocese. Then arose the question of re-naming her. Many names were suggested, and one of the Bishop's little daughters said, "call her the "Evangeline," because she will carry the Gospel." The idea was considered, and it was decided to call her by that name. Thus the pleasure yacht, under her new name, became the means of hastening forward the work of the diocese, and of conveying the Bishop to many almost inaccessible spots inhabited by settlers and native Indians.

The "Evangeline" also carries a large number of magazines, which are distributed at various points along the route. These are made up into good-sized parcels, securely tied up, so that when slipped from the side of the "Evangeline" into any passing boats, none of the contents fall out. Each parcel contains about thirty periodicals, and sometimes there are forty such parcels stored on the roof of the saloon, protected by a tarpaulin, waiting to be disposed of.

On one occasion as the "Evangeline" was steaming past a lighthouse in Lake George the Bishop said, "I wonder the people at that lighthouse content themselves with making signals, and do not row off to meet us." He then directed the deck-hand to take the boat and carry them a bundle of papers. He returned in about half-an-hour's time and reported that the men were away from home for a few hours, and the women at the lighthouse could not leave their charge to row out to meet them, but were most anxious that they should not pass without leaving them something to read. So delighted were they at receiving the papers that they gathered the few flowers that were growing in their little garden and sent them to the Bishop.

At another time, during the very hot weather, his Lordship was distributing papers amongst the men in some timber yards. These were so glad to get the bundles of literature that they gave him some ice, by means of which, in conjunction with an old box and some saw-dust, it was possible to form a primitive ice-house on board the " Evangeline."

These bundles of reading matter are much appreciated by all. Isolated dwellers will be on the look-out for the mission steamer for weeks, until at length they are rewarded by sighting her, and are cheered by a kindly message from the Bishop and the welcome parcel of magazines. And should any alteration take place in the coast line, such as the shifting of a rock, care is taken by the dwellers in the immediate neighbourhood to be even more diligent in their look-out so as to warn the Bishop of it; for in these unfrequented waters such matters do not obtain sufficient notice for him to be apprised of his danger.

But shifting rocks are not the only source of danger. To say nothing of the frequent and sudden storms, there is the danger of running into sunken trees which, having blown down in a storm, are carried by the rushing waters far out into the lakes and in time become water-logged. Then there is the ever-present danger from saw-logs, coming down the river in drives;

and if the steamer is not anchored outside the boom, there is serious danger that her sides may be crushed by the pressure of the logs against them. Still greater is the danger to a vessel if a jam has broken within two or three miles of her. But perhaps some of my readers are wondering what a "drive," a "boom," and a "jam" may be.

A "drive" is a large number of logs (trunks of trees) that have been cut down in the bush during the winter and are being carried down by the strong current of the river—swollen by the melted snows of winter—to the mills. Imagine to yourself thousands of such logs, from twelve to thirty feet in length and two or three feet in diameter, tossed about like so many matches. You will readily understand how poor a chance of escape would the "Evangeline" have, were she to find herself in the midst of such a floating timber yard, particularly if the wind were high and drove the logs against the sides.

A "boom" is a number of tree trunks joined end to end, by means of iron chains ; and the logs thus joined sometimes measure over half a mile in length. This is used to enclose the floating logs lest they should either go beyond the mill, or pass the river's mouth and be lost in the lake. Should a vessel anchor within a "boom" and logs begin to pour in unexpectedly as they often do, there is no other course but to unfasten the boom and get outside. This is attended with great danger to the men engaged in unfastening the chains, for should one of them slip off the boom, the logs would either crush him or close over him and he would be drowned.

A "jam"* is a collection of logs crowded together at some point of the river, causing a block. This generally occurs where the river is narrow or shallow. Falls and rapids are also frequent causes of jams. First a few logs are stopped, and gradually the number increases as those behind are hindered in their progress. Then the drivers (the men whose duty it is to see that all the logs duly pass down the river) have to break the jam. They spring from log to log, deafened by the noise of the rapids, and blinded by the foam; and when the log that was first jammed has been discovered, they work away with pike and cant-hook till they succeed in getting a chain round it. A team of horses is then attached to the chain and the log pulled out. This has the same effect on a jam as the removal of the keystone would have on an arch; consequently the whole jam will collapse, and all the logs rush madly down the river. It is terribly dangerous work, and each season many brave men lose their life, while engaged at it.

Who shall say that men placed so frequently in such a perilous position do not need the anxious care of a missionary; lest, in their active and dangerous life, higher things should be forgotten, and death

* See Frontispiece.

snatch them from this world unprepared for the next? It is perhaps unnecessary to say that Mr. Frost is as earnest in his ministrations to those who in his district are engaged in work of this kind as to any other members of his flock. But to return to the "Evangeline." During her ten years on Canadian waters she has had many trips, and been found invaluable. Time and again she has carried the Bishop, and rendered it possible for him to visit parts of the diocese that must otherwise have been left without his supervision.

CHAPTER IX.

The Bishop's Arrival.

When every trace of winter had disappeared, and the land had clothed itself in rich vegetation, the missionary was busily occupied in holding classes for confirmation. The Bishop was expected to make his tour early in July, and Mr. Frost was anxious that the candidates should be well prepared. Many of these candidates resided at long distances from each other, consequently a larger number of classes was necessary than is usual. This, and the bad state of many of the roads, made the work very laborious, and occupied a large amount of the missionary's time.

During the time Mr. Frost was thus engaged in preparing the young Indians for confirmation, their parents worked hard in erecting several objects of public use; a bridge was constructed in the reserve, and also a dock to provide accommodation for larger boats which might occasionally visit their settlement.

In the early part of June, an old Indian, who had for many years refused to listen to the claims of Christianity, came to Mr. Frost and wished to be baptised. When the missionary had given him a course of instruction, and assured himself of the sincerity of the Indian, he baptized him, giving him the name of Mark. At Little Current the attendances at the Church services vary much with the weather. When the weather is bad and the roads impassable, those who reside in outlying districts cannot attend; but during the summer, when the mill is working, there are a large number of people residing in the village, and these increase the congregations. At this station Mr. Frost had eight candidates for the forthcoming confirmation. Sucker Creek Reserve continued to keep up its services, and the majority of its inhabitants greatly appreciated the missionary's visits.

On July 10th, the Bishop commenced his tour. Leaving Spanish River in the "Evangeline," he steamed thirty miles to Little Current, called at the post office there, and proceeded eight miles further to fetch Mr. Frost and his tent, as he was going to hold a service at Birch Island, and then confer with the Indians about the site of a schoolhouse church, which they hoped soon to erect.

Returning from Sheguiandah, calling at Little Current for provisions, and steaming thence the remainder of the forty miles to Birch Island, took all the afternoon. It was nearly seven o'clock when having passed the narrows with its high laurentian rocks and an innumerable number of islands, with here and there a shoal, what is perhaps the most beautiful scenery in Algoma was reached.

Looking towards the main shore at the foot of a high bush-covered hill was a clearing, in front of which stood several wooden cottages, built and owned by the Indians. The principal cottage belonged to chief George. It was entirely white-washed, whilst the window sashes were painted a brilliant blue. The sun, setting opposite behind the wooded islands, was gilding the channels of water and gleaming on the windows of the chief's house. As the "Evangeline" approached, a very ragged Union Jack was hoisted in chief George's garden. In Indian settlements where there is no bell, the coming of the missionary is usually thus announced.

Notwithstanding the clouds of mosquitoes, the Bishop (who was accompanied by his daughter and two friends, one of them a lady from England, much interested in the Diocese), rowed to the landing-stage, which consisted of two trunks of trees nearly submerged, and was met by Chief George, who greeted him with courteous and friendly and yet independent bearing. As the Bishop and his party stood by the door of the Chief's house, they could see several sail-boats bringing people to the service, whilst on the right wound a path, along which the Indians were approaching. The women love bright shawls and ribbons, and the girls often plait red or green ribbons in their hair. One girl of about fourteen was holding a baby dressed in bright blue, whilst she herself was clad in a claret-coloured gown, made with pannier, velvet trimming and flounces. This looked very incongruous on that lonely island; but now that their wild animals are so diminished, the Indians are almost dependent on gifts of clothing from England and the other districts of Canada.

Having spoken to all the members of the Chief's family, the Bishop waited to say " Bou Jou " and shake hands with every individual of the congregation, which numbered about thirty. Service then took place in the Chief's house, Mr. Frost acting as interpreter during the Bishop's sermon. As the Bishop had promised to give a service at Collin's Inlet, the next day they went to Killarney, where he hoped to engage a pilot, not wishing to steer across the swell of the Georgian Bay in such a high wind. One man after another refused, but at length a young fellow undertook the duty, and they started. It was decidedly rough, but the " Evangeline " was safely brought to Collin's Inlet and moored to the wharf. The service was held at some distance from the Mission Steamer, the congregation consisting of thirty young Englishmen.

On the following day the Bishop returned to Sheguiandah. It is too shallow for the " Evangeline " to draw up to the ordinary row-boat pier, and the Indians so much appreciated the Bishop's visit, that they proposed to construct a new pier which should stretch out sufficiently far to suit the steamer on future occasions. When the Bishop and his friends went on shore, they found a young Indian planting two trees near the Church in order to commemorate the Episcopal visit. The old log church was inspected, and a visit paid to the new frame church which had recently been erected by the Indians under the missionary's instructions.

In the course of the evening Manitowasing, the Chief, brought some of his family and paid the Bishop a ceremonious visit. The Bishop made a number of enquiries with reference to the well-being of the tribe, and heard from the Chief an account of their doings since he was last among them. After a time he withdrew, and the Bishop, first spending some time writing, followed the example of the other members of his party and sought rest so as to prepare for the labours of the coming day, which were to be very heavy, and the narrative of which we will reserve for another chapter.

CHAPTER X.

A Heavy Day's Work.

Sunday, 13th July, was a very hot day, and three congregations were at different points expecting their Bishop. At each church the rite of confirmation was to be administered, necessitating an address from the Bishop as well as his sermon to the congregation generally. At 8.30 a.m. he went on shore, and by nine o'clock the Church was packed with Indians, the candidates occupying the front seats. There were about one hundred adults in the congregation, and about one-third received the Holy Communion. The deep reverence of the Indians during divine service was most impressive; there was an air of solemn earnestness pervading the assembly. The Bishop read a portion of the service and pronounced the words of confirmation in Indian over each candidate as he knelt at the rail. The Missionary, who is a fluent Indian speaker, interpreted the address and sermon sentence by sentence; he also led and accompanied the hymns on the harmonium.

The services concluded, the Bishop first shook hands with the newly confirmed, after which he stood in the middle of the church till everyone had come up to him, shaken hands and said, "Bou Jou," the

Indian version of a form of address which had been taught to their forefathers by the Jesuits, who were the pioneer missionaries in Canada.

It was now time for the Bishop and missionary to drive to the English Church, which was about two miles distant; so they started immediately, leaving the rest of the Bishop's party and Mrs. Frost to follow by water. The church being far too small for the number present, the Bishop desired that the wooden kneelers should be taken out of the pews, and placed in a double row at right angles with the pews all down the aisle. On these he requested the children to take their places, and then chairs were brought in to cover every remaining space on the floor. Even then several could not be seated, and others were unable to enter the building. The services, including Confirmation and Holy Communion ended, it was 1.30 p.m. when the Bishop started for the Parsonage.

At four o'clock the "Evangeline" left for Little Current, to which place Mr. Frost accompanied the Bishop. Here the service commenced at seven o'clock, and the church was crowded, the same arrangement for seating being adopted as at the earlier service. It was after nine before the congregation began to disperse, and the Bishop was very weary with the heat, and the exertion of delivering six addresses and sermons, besides conducting the services that day.

Monday was another very hot day. In the course of the day the English visitor was left alone on the "Evangeline." While sitting in the cabin, she saw a dark face looking in at the open door, and forgetting that she was not in England, thought a gipsy had come on board. He enquired for the Bishop, and then it transpired that the dark-haired visitor was Chief Manitowasing, of Sheguiandah. He gave the lady a letter from Chief George, of Birch Island, which he begged her to give to the Bishop, saying he would take the answer that afternoon.

The next place visited was Sucker Creek. It was necessary to drive to this place, which is situated on a hill some distance from the water. The road varied very much. At first they drove under the shadow of trees, then past a cemetery, and up a steep hill, where occasionally large pieces of rock formed part of the road. On the way up this hill a spot was pointed out where some time before an Indian woman had been murdered. Two men were known to have been with her that day; one had been drinking. Evidence was strong against him, but after a period, passed in prison, he was released. The tribe, however, with their strong sense of justice, did not acquit him, and he was expelled from the settlement, so strong was the feeling on the question. Later in the day they came to a much pleasanter point, where, overlooking a lovely stretch of bay, stood a large wooden farm-house with barn and fence, and flourishing fields around.

On they went, and at last reached the Indian reserve of Sucker Creek. Here there are small neat cottages, and close beside the clearings; "bush" surrounds them on every side. Here and there a magnificent fir-tree, whilst birch and other feathery trees wave above a luxuriant under-growth. The scarlet berries of the elder, and the bright green of delicate ferns were most refreshing to the travellers after their hot drive over a rough road.

At Sucker Creek there was no saw-mill or other industry by which the Indians could earn wages, yet they were found to be learning the meaning of self-help, and working industriously at their clearings and in their gardens. The houses which the Indians built for themselves were substantial and clean, whilst all the grown people of the tribe were neat and respectable looking. The appearance of children varied very much, some were wearing white frocks and had their hair plaited, while others were looking very untidy and dirty.

The service was held in the schoolhouse and was attended by about forty adults and ten children, some of the Indians, including the Chief, being away from home. In the middle of the room in which the service was held, stood a stove, and on this was placed a bright tin can of water and a clean glass. From time to time during the service some member of the congregation would quietly glide to the stove, and dipping the tumbler into the water, quench her thirst.

The little building in which they assembled served for the double purpose of Church and Schoolhouse, and was built by the Indians, who had a great love for it. Nowhere could there have been more devout communicants than the two sets who approached the Holy Table that Monday. The Indians have a curious way of waiting about before the service begins. At Sucker Creek, on this occasion, when the Bishop and Mr. Frost had arrived and everything was ready, the Indians were grouped outside and waiting. The Bishop went to some little boys who had come into the church, and heard them each repeat the Lord's Prayer in Ojibway; afterwards he went to the girls who recited the Apostles' Creed. The Indians still remaining outside, the Bishop and missionary sat down and waited. After a few remarks had been exchanged between the principal men of Sucker Creek and Chief Manitowasing of Sheguiandah, the bell was rung for a minute, the congregation trooped in, and service commenced. The men sat on the north side of the aisle, the women on the south, with the children in front.

As is the custom on week-days, the Bishop made a little speech when the service was concluded. He congratulated the Indians on the progress made in their farming, and told them how pleased he felt at knowing how nicely their children had learnt the Lord's Prayer and the Creed. He said that he had brought an English visitor who took much interest in the welfare of the Indians, as well as in seeing the country. He then introduced the English lady to them, and an Indian woman came up and shook hands with her, and said something by way of welcome.

It was then suggested that the Birch Island Indians should spend a day at Sheguiandah, the Bishop promising to fetch them in the "Evangeline," from Little Current. Manitowasing was asked if he should like the Indians of Birch Island to have a picnic with his band at Sheguiandah, and he replied that he should not only like it, but that if it were decided on, he would receive his friends the night before, and do all in his power for their comfort.

After each Indian had said "Bou Jou" and shaken hands with the Bishop, they shook hands with the lady from England. Outside the building they waited to discuss a question with the Bishop and missionary, and it was surprising to see the vivid interest evinced by different members of the groups and the rapid way in which arguments were brought forward on both sides. The next day the Bishop proceeded to Little Current; where, after seeing his daughter and her friends into a steamer bound for Sault Sainte Marie, he continued his Manitoulin visitation, which covered an entire month.

CHAPTER XI.

An Indian Picnic.

The suggestion that the Indians of Birch Island should visit those of Sheguiandah was carried out in August. The day was beautifully fine, a perfect summer's day, and the clear waters of the lake sparkled in the warm sunlight as the Bishop and Mrs. Sullivan arrived at Little Current. The Bishop, true to his promise, had come in the " Evangeline " to fetch the Indians and convey them to Sheguiandah. A large number from the neighbouring reserve were taken on board and in due time the vessel arrived safely at its destination.

Among the guests were two Indian chiefs, who were accompanied by their daughters, dark, handsome women, with very beautiful eyes and a wealth of raven hair. They all entered with delight into the day's proceedings, and it was pleasant to notice the wonderful play of expression upon the countenances of the two chiefs as they entered into a most animated conversation ; all the more pleasant on account of its rarity, for as a rule these Indian chiefs are most undemonstrative.

The chiefs' daughters wore dresses of brilliant colour, and each had a shawl of even brighter hue.

Most of the Indian girls present were also clothed in very bright colours, for which they have at all times a great fondness.

The proceedings commenced with a short service in the church which was nicely decorated for the occasion. The village street had also been made bright and gay in honour of the event. The Bishop addressed a few words to the assembled Indians, speaking on the many advantages and blessings of social intercourse and friendliness; he expressed a hope that the gathering would be productive of good as well as of pleasure.

After the service was over dinner was prepared. Elaborate arrangements were made for this important part of the proceedings. A suitable place having been found in the bush near by, the spot was cleared by the Indians and a flag hoisted. Tables and seats were arranged in position and everything was found ready. The Bishop had kindly undertaken to provide the necessary refreshments, and an ample supply was provided. When grace had been said, the feast commenced. At this most interesting point of the proceedings a photograph of the group was taken.

When the dinner was ended, various amusements were indulged in, such as races and jumping competitions. The Bishop had brought with him a large number of prizes with which he rewarded those who entered for the different events. Both men and

AN INDIAN PICNIC.

AN INDIAN PICNIC.

women entered for the races, and prizes were generally presented to those who were unsuccessful as well as to those who were successful. The jumping especially afforded the greatest amusement to the whole party, and the laughter was hearty and prolonged. Everyone who took part in these games was satisfied, because, as the Indians themselves confessed, "Everybody received a prize, the losers as well as the winners."

When the athletic contests were concluded, the Bishop again addressed the Indians, and the proceedings were at length brought to an end by the singing of "God save the Queen" sung in Ojibway. Any food that remained from the dinner was distributed to those Indians who most needed it; then the gathering broke up, everyone having thoroughly enjoyed "The best picnic they had ever seen" as the Indians quaintly expressed it.

In the evening the Bishop returned to Little Current, taking the Indians of that neighbourhood back to their homes. He then proceeded to Spanish River, and anchored opposite to the Indian village. Very few of the Indians were absent in the bush, so on the following morning a service was held, rendered in the Indian tongue. In the course of his address the Bishop dwelt upon the terrible consequences which the atrocious trade in "Firewater" would bring upon the Indians if not avoided. After the service the Bishop, who was negociating the purchase of some potatoes, took several women and children on board the " Evangeline " and gave them a short excursion up the river, while the men were busily engaged in digging the required quantity of potatoes.

Meanwhile the missionary visited a village or settlement of Indians at a place which was encumbered with the unprepossessing name of Ogahmeekunaung. The district known by this name is a narrow neck of land with a bay on either side, where for many years a portage path has existed for the convenience of Indians and others navigating the inner channel with their canoes. The village is built on both sides of the portage road, the greater number of houses being situated on the Western Bay. The bays and channels are studded with islands of every shape and size, picturesque and well wooded, which afford a variety of lovely scenery possibly unsurpassed by any in Canada. For many years the Indians lived at a place some distance from the village, but they abandoned it because many had died there; they therefore decided to build a new village, and in many ways the move was advantageous. At Ogahmeekunaung they are nearer their gardens, they are nearer their firewood, and what is still more important, the place affords a better harbour for their boats.

Many years before they moved to their present abode, the missionary was in the habit of visiting them from time to time, when he would hold a service in one of their houses. Within a year or so of the missionary's present visit, several efforts had been made to build a schoolhouse, yet nothing definite had been accomplished, although some logs were hewn and carted to the site of the proposed new building. But during the summer of which we are now writing a neat little building was erected. The expenses were met partly by donations from the Indians, and partly by a grant from the Indian Department of the Canadian Government; the labour was supplied by the Indians themselves under the supervision of the missionary.

This building, which serves the purpose of both church and school, has lancet windows and a porch; the inside is lined with narrow strips of matchboarding, and the arched ceiling is covered with the same material. In appearance it is quite ecclesiastical, and the whole work reflects great credit on the Indians who built it. Two handsome chandeliers and some bracket lamps, the gift of a friend, form an ornament to the interior. The Indians, previous to a service, scrub the floor till it becomes a glistening white. All the services held in this building since its completion, have been attended by large congregations, sometimes every inhabitant of the village being present. Amongst these there are a large number of communicants. During his visit Mr. Frost held a service, and had every reason to be satisfied with the condition of the station.

CHAPTER XII.

AUNDAGWAHMENEKAUNING.

During the early part of the winter the Indians at Aundagwahmenekauning had been improving their church, and its better appearance and arrangements certainly repaid them for the labour and care they had bestowed upon the building. When it was first erected about six years previously, it was a rather rough and irregular log structure, yet serviceable and airy. It was exceedingly well ventilated—too much so in fact, for the air used to blow rather freely through the cracks of the gables. But with all its faults and drawbacks it was a great improvement on the old shanty that had for some years previously served as a church. The lancet windows, with their small quantity of stained glass, looked more ecclesiastical than the little square windows of the shanty; and the three-quarter roof was more church-like than the flat roof with which the shanty was covered.

But more important than all these external improvements, the log church was larger and furnished with seats, holy table and pulpit, so that the services could be conducted in a more orderly manner than was possible in the discarded shanty.

AUNDAGWAHMENEKAUNING.

Such was the state of the building, when the Indians commenced the work of improvement. In this state it had continued for several years, for the Indians of Aundagwahmenekauning advance slowly and with caution, and consider undue haste to be undignified. But now at length the work was taken in hand and carried out in a satisfactory manner.

First of all the gables were battened; and next a bell was purchased and hung in a suitable position. The ringing of the bell made it unnecessary for the missionary to blow his horn as he passed through the village to assemble the people for service; which custom had prevailed hitherto. The bell was a great improvement, for it could be heard all over the village, whereas formerly those people who lived beyond the church in the opposite direction to that in which the missionary was approaching, did not hear the horn he blew on his way to church. The next step in the way of improvement involved more labour and expense. A quantity of good matchboarding was procured and the interior of the church very neatly lined. This was a heavy undertaking, and the entire band of Indians for several days worked very diligently until it was completed. When this was finished a small vestry was built, and a new stove placed in the church.

Then, when so much that was really necessary had been done, an organ was added; not new by any means, and slightly out of tune, but for all that a useful and much valued addition. The last work of improvement was the boarding of the outside of the church, so that its character of a log building was entirely concealed both inside and out. The appearance was then still further improved by painting the window frames and door.

Christmas at Ogahmeekunaung was a very bright and happy season, as indeed it is at most places; the chief feature of the gaiety was a Christmas tree entertainment which took place in the Schoolhouse. A balsam tree was found and decorated with tapers, and then from its branches were suspended candies and cakes, toys and dolls, which had been sent to the village a few days before.

This was the first Christmas tree ever seen in the place, and was described as a unique affair bearing all manner of fruits. It was a very pretty sight to see the little Indian girls feasting their eyes on the dolls in a sort of rapt ecstasy. But most unfortunately there were more little girls to admire and long for the dolls than dolls to bestow; consequently those who received the coveted prizes were very happy, and the rest were sadly disappointed. One poor woman who was present had several things given to her to take home to her children, who were unable to come. An old man got a coat, another old Indian a warm overcoat, and everyone received a present of some kind. The children feasted on cake and candies, and much useful clothing was distributed amongst them, including caps, and socks, frocks, and coats, and many other useful articles.

These gifts were all the more acceptable because some of the Indians were very poor that winter. Their potatoes were frozen in the pit, for the frost had come before the snow which usually protects them; they had been unsuccessful in their autumn fishing, and therefore fish was scarce; and to make matters worse, there were very few partridges and rabbits in the woods, with which they might replenish their stock of provisions.

At Aundagwahmenekauning there was also a Christmas tree, similar to the one at Ogahmeekunaung. "Santa Claus," impersonated by an intelligent young Indian, formed the great feature of the proceedings at Sheguiandah and produced much fun and laughter. At this time many of the older women at Sheguiandah were liberally provided with warm clothing.

Many of the articles distributed were sent to Mr. Frost by the Bishop, who had received them from the "Algoma Association for Prayer and Work in Union with the Diocese of Algoma." This is an association which has branches in London and some of the counties and towns in England, and whose Central Secretary resides at 9, Carlton Road, Ealing, London, W. These workers are, in their own quiet way, doing what they can to forward the church's work in this missionary diocese, and we are sure that any of the associates would be glad to give such information as they may possess, should any reader care to ask for it.

The bales containing the clothing were sent to the Diocese from England through the Colonial and Continental Church Society, who in addition to their other and still more substantial aid, kindly paid the freight charges upon them.

What does not the Church in Algoma owe to the great Church Societies in England? The society just mentioned provides a large part of the stipends of a fifth of the clergy of the Diocese. Then there is the Society for the Propagation of the Gospel in Foreign Parts. How largely does that venerable society help in matter of stipends of the clergy, the episcopal endowment fund, and the maintenance of the "Evangeline." Three-fourths of the present number of the clergy are on its list of accredited representatives, drawing their stipends largely from the Society.

Then there is the Society for Promoting Christian Knowledge. Besides their large grant to the Episcopal Endowment Fund, this society is ever ready to respond to petitions for assistance in church building, wherever their eminently reasonable conditions are complied with. There is scarce a church in the whole of the Diocese which, if it does not owe its very existence to that grand society, at all events has received a large grant towards its erection, and, in a word been completed by it. Where again would the various Sunday School libraries be without the aid so liberally extended to them by it? To say nothing of the wholesale grants of Bibles, prayer-books and hymn-books, readily voted for the use of steamers plying to and fro on the great inland seas within the Diocese, thus "Casting bread upon the waters" which beyond a doubt will be found again, though it may be in some cases "After many days." Verily indeed these societies are rightly called the great nursing mothers of the church. But

Nos............ non haec dicere.
Conamur, tenues grandia. HOR. CARM i., 6.

CHAPTER XIII.

Spring.

During the winter the missionary made several journeys to the distant stations of the mission. He had been compelled to purchase a new horse, which he found most useful and a great help in his work. Till the ice became sound he was unable to go very far from home, and so confined his work to the four stations on the Manitoulin Island. It was early in January before he could make use of his horse and sleigh, and the first journey was to Birch Island and White Fish River, including some of the camps on Long Lake. Many interesting services were held among the Indians in the reserve, and some gifts of clothing were distributed, which had been sent by the ladies of the Woman's Auxiliary. These gifts, as well as the services which were held, were much appreciated by the Indians. The following week a visit was paid to La Cloche and Spanish River, where a large congregation of Indians assembled in the schoolhouse. On his return journey the missionary visited a lumber camp, picturesquely situated on the shores of a lake, and was heartily welcomed by the men who were working there.

MR. FROST TRAVELLING.

The next journey was down the Georgian Bay, calling at Killarney, where Mr. Frost held a service. Next day he reached Collin's Inlet and found the population of that village had greatly diminished during the winter; only seventeen persons attended the service that was held in the schoolhouse. He also visited a camp situated on a lake about half-way between Killarney and Sudbury, and a day later arrived at Beaverstone. During the earlier part of the winter a new road had been made through the woods, and by making use of this, Mr. Frost was enabled to avoid that piece of bad ice where his horse had been so unfortunate the previous winter. Many lumber camps were visited during this tour, and many services held, the attendances at which frequently numbered over a hundred. The Indians at Gromline Point were not forgotten, and a service was held in the house of an Indian named Kahgahguns.

On the next day, which was Sunday, the weather was very rough; but notwithstanding the difficulties of travelling, the missionary managed to hold services at three different places, the last place reached being Collin's Inlet. On the Monday Mr. Frost visited a camp where the majority of the people were French. These attended the service, and listened to the address with great interest. They afterwards gave the missionary a pair of mocassins (shoes made of soft leather, largely used by the Indians and others for travelling over the snow). The next day Mr.

Frost set out on his homeward journey, but the weather was so bad and the ice in such an unsafe condition, that very little progress could be made. On the morrow he fell in with some travellers who were going in the same direction as himself, and by nightfall they reached Killarney. It was a most laborious journey; at one time the distance traversed in five hours was only nine miles. After staying the night at Killarney, Mr. Frost arrived at his home in Sheguiandah the following day.

After this, two visits were paid to White Fish River and services held both among the Indians and white people of that settlement. During the first visit to the place the missionary remained a week and held a service every evening. Altogether about two hundred persons attended these week-day services. On the second occasion there was a large gathering of Indians in the new church, and there was a celebration of the Holy Communion. At this service some Indians were present who had come all the way from Sheguiandah and Sucker Creek. Spanish River was the next place visited, and having held a service there, the missionary journeyed still further up the river to see a poor woman who had been very ill. He held a service in the house and celebrated the Holy Communion. Meanwhile the bright festival of Easter was approaching, and Mr. Frost hastened back to the mission stations on the islands. During Holy Week service was held every evening; three were held on Good Friday, and five on Easter Day. This was a very trying day for Mr. Frost, commencing with an early celebration at seven o'clock. The last evening service was held at a station some distance from Sheguiandah, and owing to the bad state of the roads, it was midnight before the missionary reached home. Some of the services that day were attended by Indians from the north shore, and in all there were about fifty communicants. Throughout the season of spring the Indians were very busy putting in their crops of corn, wheat, oats, peas, and potatoes, nor did these occupations interfere with their regular attendance at the services which were held from time to time in the different settlements. During the period of which we are writing the number of cattle on the reserve largely increased, but there was a decided tendency to get rid of the oxen and keep horses in preference. In some instances, however, oxen were found to be more useful for work on their farms. Several new houses, larger and more convenient than their old cabins, were built, around many of which were trim little gardens enclosed by a neat picket fence; thus the appearance of the village was greatly improved. The missionary discovered that amongst the women it was usual to make a regular cleaning day of Saturday, and anyone neglecting to make her house clean and bright for Sunday was considered particularly heathenish.

About this time the missionary paid a visit to the Indians at Aundagwahmenekauning and found several of them absent from home, having obtained employment at a camp some distance off. Here there were one or two fairly large cottages having outside sheds which were used as kitchens during the summer. Some cottages contained only one room, but all were exceptionally clean and neat.

As Mr. Frost was now able to make use of his boat, he went to see the Indians at Ogahmeekunaung and held a service in the little church there, which was attended by nearly the whole population of the village. Here he found, that although the Indians took much delight in their gardening operations, the gardens themselves did not seem to be particularly flourishing. However some gardens that were situated at a distance from the village, appeared to be doing better, and their products well repaid the care that had been bestowed upon them. Many of the Indians here were engaged at this time in fishing.

Leaving Ogahmeekunaung the missionary next visited Subing, and a large congregation assembled at the service he held there. Although the Indians of Subing live chiefly by hunting, they possess gardens and grow corn and potatoes, but they are not as yet very successful in their agricultural pursuits. When Mr. Frost had completed his visits to these and other outlying stations, he hastened to his home at Sheguiandah, as he was expecting that the Bishop would shortly make his annual visit to the island.

CHAPTER XIV.

AN EPISCOPAL VISITATION.

This annual visit of the Bishop of Algoma to the Sheguiandah Mission duly took place. Accompanied by Mr. Frost, his Lordship visited the homes of the Indians in Sheguiandah village, and expressed the pleasure he felt on seeing the improvements that had been made in many of the houses since his last visit to them a year before. The Indians were delighted with their visitor, and with the kind words addressed to many of them. On Sunday the Bishop preached in St. Andrew's Church and a very large congregation, consisting almost entirely of Indians, listened to his sermon with great attention. Then followed the confirmation service, the candidates being a young man and his wife. Many Indians and the few white people that were in the congregation remained for the celebration of Holy Communion which followed the confirmation. When the morning services were over the Bishop had a drive of eleven miles to Sucker Creek, and preached in the Indian church, where the service was announced to commence at three o'clock. The Indians listened very attentively to the Bishop's address and thanked him for it when the service was over. Here the church was prettily decorated with flowers and vine leaves in honour of the event. Then followed another drive, and in the evening at seven o'clock the Bishop officiated at the Church of Holy Trinity at Little Current. The sermon was based on the text, "Whatsoever ye would that men should to you, do ye also to them." The next day an old Indian remarked, "That was good advice that the Bishop gave the people, if they will only mind and act on it." Besides this service and sermon there was also a celebration of the Holy Communion at Little Current. After the evening service the Bishop drove back to Sheguiandah very tired after all his exertions.

On Monday morning the Bishop and Mr. Frost started for Birch Island in the missionary's little sailing boat, taking with them a man to help. There was little or no wind to help them along, so rowing was the order of the day for the first ten miles, and for parts of the last ten; the Bishop taking his share. Birch Island was reached at eight o'clock in the evening; a camp fire was lighted, and supper cooked and eaten on the shore. The repast was spread on a box, stones being used for seats. The Bishop appeared much pleased with the success of the meal. The night was spent in the garret of an unfinished house; fortunately it had a roof, for it was pouring with rain all night. Next morning breakfast was obtained at a fish house close by; and then the Bishop held a service in the new church.

AN EPISCOPAL VISITATION.

This church, a frame structure built on stone pillars, was quite a model of Indian architecture, for it had both been designed and built by the Indians. The Bishop, who had not seen it before, was very much pleased with it. The services connected with the opening of this church were of a most interesting character. Indians had gathered from all parts to be present; upwards of a hundred managed to crowd into the building, but others were unable to gain admission. Among the ceremonies of the day was the presentation to the Indians of a new flag. The Bishop when in England had addressed a small drawing-room meeting in a country house in Sussex, and had told his hearers that the Indians were very loyal and would like a Union Jack, not only to show their allegiance to their great mother the Queen, but also to hoist on Sundays as a signal for divine service, for these Indians did not possess a bell. Before the Bishop left England a flag was entrusted to him to be delivered to the chief; and it was this Union Jack that was now presented to the Birch Island Indians. In the afternoon the Bishop and Mr. Frost sailed to La Cloche, a village on the north shore, about sixteen miles off. As the wind was very favourable they reached their destination about six o'clock, and encamped for the night in an empty house at the deserted Hudson Bay Post. The Bishop slept on the floor with some rugs under him.

Next morning, having breakfasted at half-past five, a start was made for the Indian village on the Spanish river. First a portage of a mile, then the canoe for three miles, then another portage of a mile, then a paddle in the canoe for a mile across the lake, then a walk of a mile and a half brought the Bishop and the missionary to the schoolhouse at Spanish River. They found John Esquimaux and other Indians building a turret for a new bell which had lately been presented to them. The missionary examined five candidates for confirmation, who had been prepared by John Esquimaux the catechist, and finding their replies to his questions were satisfactory, presented them to the Bishop to be confirmed. Service was held at twelve o'clock and included an address from the Bishop. Here also there was a celebration of Holy Communion at which there were thirteen communicants. These services were not concluded till half-past two, when the Bishop and Mr. Frost returned by the same route as they had travelled in the morning, reaching La Cloche at eight o'clock, much fatigued by the day's work and tiring journey. After breakfast next morning at half-past six o'clock they started on the return journey to Sheguiandah in the sailing boat. The voyage took eight hours, for the wind was very unfavourable. The next day the Bishop had intended to leave Sheguiandah for Gore Bay, but the steamer by which he had hoped to go passed without calling,

PORTAGING.

so he was compelled to stay another night with Mr. Frost.

The next morning Mr. Frost drove him to Manitowaning to catch a steamer there. This was his lordship's last chance. He caught the steamer, however, and after a sleepless night, was up by half-past six next morning. Having breakfasted, he was driven by Mr. McLeod, the resident missionary, to one of his out-stations, Kagawong, twelve miles distant from Gore Bay. The return journey was taken in the afternoon under a broiling sun. There was no shade and much of the road was corduroy— a road made by placing trunks of trees across a given track. Such a road is usually made through swamps, and would be built in the following manner. First the tops and smaller limbs of the trees are thrown into the swamp, thus forming a foundation, upon which are placed three or more lengths of tree trunks running parallel with the road. These act as sleepers upon which other tree trunks are rolled and placed at right angles to the road. The roadway is now complete, and we will leave it to the reader to imagine the amount of comfort to be got out of a drive of twelve miles over such a road under a burning sun, the wheels bumping from one tree trunk to another.

CHAPTER XV.

Delays.

Towards the end of the month of November Mr. Frost left home and paid a prolonged visit to the most distant parts of his mission. It had not been his intention to stay from home such a length of time when he first started on his journey, but bad weather and other causes detained him on the route. Many hindrances had occurred to prevent his taking this journey earlier in the autumn, and he had been obliged to postpone it from week to week.

When at length an opportunity presented itself and he was able to leave Sheguiandah, he embarked on a steamboat for the first part of his journey, fearing to venture in his own boat as the weather was very rough. At the first place where the steamer called, Mr. Frost was detained two days; he made good use of this time, visiting amongst the inhabitants. Then he secured a passage in the steamer for the next village, where he stayed several days, visiting during the day-time, and holding services in the schoolhouse every evening. He was invited to visit the day school and was glad to take this opportunity of addressing the children.

On Sunday morning he held a service and in the afternoon he rowed down to a shanty where several men were living and gave them a service. He was enabled to do this owing to the kindness of a friend in lending him a skiff. In the evening he visited a camp in the neighbourhood and held a service. This camp was about two miles distant from the village and was approached by a road through the woods, so muddy and soft as to be almost impassable. Along this road the missionary advanced as best he could, the heavy rain beating on his face, and greatly adding to his discomfort. Still he persevered and it proved to be a most timely visit to the camp, for the men had had no opportunity of meeting together for public worship since they left for the "limit" some weeks before.

And what is a "limit"? asks the reader. We will explain. It is a tract of land often many miles square, on which the employer of the men has obtained from the government the sole right to cut the pine or other trees designated in his license. About September (the season regulating the movements to a great extent) the men leave the mills, which are generally situated near the mouths of the rivers or on the lakes, and journey, either up the course of the river or along the shore of the lake as the case may be, until they come to the "limit." Here they are joined by other men, representatives of many different nations often meeting in the same camp. Here through the long dreary months of winter they are housed either in shanties or camps.

H

At break of day they are up and off to their labours, and until sundown may be heard the clear ring of the axe as it bites into the trees; and ever and anon a thundering crash as some lord of the forest bends its lofty crest and falls prostrate upon the earth. The work is hard, fearfully hard, the days are long and monotonous; Sunday is too often little different from other days to men in such isolation, except that they do no work. And were it not for the fact that usually a number of godly men may be found among them, Sunday would soon become not only a day of unholy rest, but one which would bring untold harm both to the men themselves, and also to those who reside anywhere near a camp. O how they need the ministrations of the Church, and what opportunity for sowing the seed of eternal life is here. Mr. Frost was not the man to let such a chance pass by unheeded. That night, first by a service and afterwards by individual counsel he did his utmost for their spiritual welfare. He shared one of the most comfortable bunks for the night, and the next morning, after breakfasting with the men, he retraced his steps to the village.

The next place visited was on the banks of a small river, whose current was too swift for the skiff, so the missionary walked along the river bank till he reached the village. After making a short stay here he pushed on to an Indian village which was approached by a road on which the water stood knee deep in places. He lost his way several times, for it is difficult to follow a trail over rocks and through water; however, he reached the village at last and held a service there both in the afternoon, and again in the evening. The church was well filled with Indians, and after the service was over, several came to the missionary and enquired after their friends who lived in the neighbourhood of Sheguiandah. Some Indians were present who came from a place far back in the bush beyond the height of land.

On the following morning Mr. Frost retraced his steps and found that the depth of water on the road had been increased by a fall of snow during the night. His next station was reached by hard rowing against a strong wind, but not before he had been delayed two days on the route by bad weather. In consequence of this delay he lost the steamboat by which he had hoped to return to Sheguiandah. Unfortunately, just before the next steamer called at the village, the frost set in, and the captain, fearing he might meet with some accident or be frozen in, abandoned the voyage. So Mr. Frost was compelled to make his way home to Sheguiandah, partly by canoe and partly by crossing the ice where it was of sufficient thickness.

In due time Christmas returned and was honoured in the Mission in the usual manner; bright, hearty services and Christmas tree entertainments. During the winter Mr. Frost occupied much of his time in going from camp to camp holding services and generally administering to the denizens of the forest.

At length the frost began to yield to the increasing heat of the sun, and the Indians prepared for their usual camping out in the sugar bush. Easter came, and those Indians who were temporarily living in the sugar bush flocked back to Sheguiandah to be present at the services. On Easter Day there was an early celebration of the Holy Communion at seven o'clock, attended by a large number of communicants. The next service began at nine o'clock. A large congregation listened to the missionary's sermon on the subject of the Resurrection with deep attention, and joined in heartily singing the joyous Easter hymns. During this service an interesting ceremony took place. The old Chief Manitowahsing was presented with a license from the Bishop of Algoma authorising him to act as lay reader and catechist in the mission. The next day the chief wrote the following letter to the Bishop:

"GREAT BLACK COAT,—

I will try to teach and help my people, acting on the authority which you give to me in the license, if the Saviour help me. It is in His strength that we are strong. Also it was for no small reason that I asked from you your seal. It was seriously, for the sake of the truth. I would like to ask you to intercede for me with the Lord, that I may be strengthened for this work. I am not such a good scholar as some are, yet I trust that I know the truth in my heart. I send my greetings in the Lord Jesus.—I am your obedient servant,

     ARTHUR MANITOWAHSING."

At St. Peter's Church, Sheguiandah, there was a celebration of the Holy Communion and a sermon at eleven o'clock. A good congregation assembled, but the number of communicants was not so large as at the early service. At the Indian church, Sucker Creek, service was held at three o'clock in the afternoon, and in the evening a large congregation met at Little Current.

CHAPTER XVI.

Gore Bay.

Gore Bay is a pretty and clean little village on the Great Manitoulin Island containing about five hundred inhabitants. It is pleasantly situated in a sheltered bay and nestles between cliffs some two hundred feet in height. These cliffs are covered with pine and other trees and protect both the western and eastern sides of the village. Towards the south stretches some of the finest farming land in the country, upon which are built here and there some very comfortable homesteads with large barns and other farm buildings. The scene presented to the eye of a traveller as he views it on some fine spring morning is a beautiful one; with its silver streams and its soft delicious haze holding the outpoured light in folds of colour. The rich shades of the growing crops; the snowy sheep as they pasture, the lowing cattle as they graze, all speak of comfort, and form a picture worthy of an artist's brush.

Gore Bay has its resident clergyman, who has also under his charge as out stations, Kagawong, the Township of Mills, Silver Water, Sheshewaning, and other places in the vicinity. The total number of souls living within this district, which is ecclesiastically known as the mission of Gore Bay, is about twelve hundred. The resident clergyman is the Rev. J. H. McLeod, who informs us that a large proportion of the total population are members of the Church of England. The church at Gore Bay is dedicated to All Saints; the congregation here is a good one, but the present building is old, and too small for it. The church family are contemplating the erection of a new church, and they are doing their utmost to erect it with as little outside aid as possible. They have also resolved to raise the necessary funds without resorting to such modern methods as bazaars, entertainments and the like; to which, when held for the purpose of obtaining funds for church building, both the missionary and his people have a great dislike.

In a letter received a few days before these words were written, Mr. McLeod says they have been so successful that the whole of the material is now on the site, and what is more to the point, all the necessary funds to meet the estimated cost of erecting the church, have been subscribed, with the exception of about fifty dollars.

We have already said that the services at All Saints are attended by large congregations. These congregations often include members of many different religious denominations, and in the summer season a number of tourists, who make Gore Bay their temporary home, swell the already overflowing congregation.

When the Bishop visited Gore Bay in August, 1892, he confirmed a class of fifteen candidates all of whom afterwards received the Holy Communion and shewed (to use the Bishop's own words) " by the devoutness of their demeanour and in some cases by tears coursing down their cheeks how deeply they realised the solemnity of the vows they had taken."

In the Township of Mills, the church is dedicated to St. James. It is a log church and was built entirely by the settlers themselves. It is now in a very serviceable condition, for they have recently very much improved it, doing the work by means of their own unaided exertions. The congregations often assemble in such numbers that many have to be content with worshipping outside the building, the church being too small to give even standing room to all.

Kagawong, or Mudge Bay, as it is sometimes called, is situated about twelve miles from Gore Bay. There is no church here and the congregation have to content themselves with the use of a public hall, in which Mr. McLeod is permitted to hold a service on alternate Sundays so long as he arranges the hours of service so as not to clash with the use of the hall by other bodies. The congregation here is a hearty one, so much so indeed that the missionary especially mentions the heartiness with which they sing and respond. It is to be hoped that they will soon see their way to move in the matter of church building, and we will hope that at no distant date they may have a church of their own in which to worship.

Mr. McLeod is a hard-working and painstaking missionary, and he is ably assisted in his work by his most excellent wife; and as a natural consequence both are not only respected by the whole community but by many are deeply loved. At all times he is ready to undergo any amount of self-denial, from time to time, leaving his home early on a Tuesday morning and not returning until the following Sunday evening in time for service. On such occasions he holds a service each evening at some different place, and on the Sunday he holds three. He is obliged to keep two ponies, for one alone would be quite unable to stand the continuous work. From this it will be gathered that he spends a considerable part of his life "in journeyings oft," and these journeys are very frequently not over the best of roads particularly in spring and autumn.

Then there are no hotels in the places where he visits, in which, after his day's work, he may seek such rest as they can offer. But instead thereof he has to seek it where best he can; often enough in some small shanty, whose walls and roof are alike, of one material, logs. The sole accommodation of these shanties is one room, with a partition, reaching sometimes up to the rafters, at others not so high, thus forming a second apartment. When staying in a shanty the more comfortable of the two apartments is given to the missionary, but what rest is he likely to find should there be, as in nine cases out of ten there are, young children passing a restless night on the other side of the partition. For children in Canada are much the same as they are in England, and occasionally amuse themselves with screaming. just by way of trying the strength of their lungs. If the missionary has not learnt to sleep through disturbances he will probably learn to do so before he has long been engaged at such work.

At another of Mr. McLeod's out-stations the only building available for service is a public hall, and as it has no windows or other openings save the door, all the light has to come in through the open door. At a service in this hall some time ago, a poor old man was among the worshippers. He had no book, but even if he had had one, the bad light and his aged eyes would have rendered it useless. Nor did he require one either, for as a boy and youth, when in the old country, he had so regularly attended divine service, that he knew the whole service by heart. And now, after the lapse of years he again heard the old familiar words, and once again with as much heartiness as his agitation allowed—joined in the responses and other parts of the service. And as he prayed, the tears coursed down his cheeks. The missionary saw, and felt that he was repaid for many a day's hard labour, and understood still more clearly how great is the privilege thus to serve while he waits.

CHAPTER XVII.

BIRCH ISLAND.

There was a large gathering of Indians on Birch Island on the occasion of the Bishop's annual visit to the Sheguiandah Mission. The Bishop had promised the Indians a picnic when he was visiting them the year before, and he now arrived from Little Current to find about two hundred of them, all members of the Church of England. They had come with their families and fishing boats from Sheguiandah, Spanish River and Sucker Creek to take part in the proceedings.

The scene on the island was a very picturesque one, the flag beside the chief's dwelling was flying mast high in honour of the Bishop's visit, the canvas tents were pitched along the shore; birch bark wigwams were erected by those who were not fortunate enough to possess tents, and a fleet of fishing boats were moored close by. The arrival of the "Big Black Coat" was announced by the firing of guns, while several boats came out to meet him, and to exchange the usual "Bou Jou."

The little church was far too small to accommodate all the Indians, so it was necessary to find a roomy place in which to hold a service. An adjacent island was selected for this purpose, and benches were arranged in a shady spot admirably adapted for an outdoor service. Soon the " Evangeline " bell rang out its summons, and in a little while the bay was a scene of the liveliest bustle as the boats skimmed over it, each bringing its living cargo to the appointed place of meeting. The Groves have been called " God's Great Temples," and here was a return to the primitive usage.

There, in the softened light of the setting sun, Bishop and missionary stood face to face with two hundred swarthy denizens of the forest, once ignorant worshippers of the great " Manitou," now baptised believers in Christ, and as devout and reverent in their demeanour as the members of any congregation in any of our cities. Every head was uncovered, every eye turned to the ground. Some hymns were sung in Ojibway with great heartiness, and included such familiar ones as " Jesu, Lover of my Soul," and " There is a Happy Land."

The service consisted of a portion of evening prayer, while the Bishop's sermon, interpreted by Mr. Frost, told them of God's love and goodness, first and most of all in the gift of His Son, and then in all their family blessings ; the fish in the waters, the deer in the forest, the fruits in the earth, waiting to reward the tiller's toil. Then the Bishop emphasised the blessings of education for their children, provided for them in the Indian homes, of which as yet they have been slow to avail themselves, owing largely to their great affection for their children, and their unwillingness to see them go away, and secondly to the fact that a few years ago two or three girls and boys died at the home, and these poor simple Indians have not yet recovered from the superstitious dread that the "Mujji-Mukuedoo," the evil spirit, hovered about them.

The confirmation of Chief Shoobekishik and his wife, from Spanish River, formed a very interesting feature in this service. The service closed with another Indian hymn and the Benediction. By this time the hour for their evening meal had come, and very soon the little fleet of fishing boats was seen scudding over the water again, bearing them back to their tents and wigwams.

At eight o'clock next morning there was a celebration of the Holy Communion in the little church, when upwards of fifty Indians communicated. There is a quiet subdued solemnity of deportment which invariably characterises the Indian in all his acts of worship, and this was especially observable that morning.

Breakfast followed shortly after, and then several hours were devoted to a variety of games, into which competitors of all ages and of both sexes entered with the greatest zest—running, jumping, putting the weight, canoe races, sail boat races, and many other amusements. The prizes were simple, consisting of useful articles of dress for the girls, and for the others of candies, knives, fishing lines and hooks, and cakes of scented soap.

When the races were over the usual " Pow-wow " meeting was held, at which the question of the school and the appointment of a new teacher occupied much time. When the " Pow-wow " was over the hour for departure had arrived, but in view of the stormy weather outside, the Bishop postponed his return to Little Current till the morning.

On the morrow everyone was astir by five o'clock, on board the "Evangeline," fires were lighted and steam up. Anchor was soon weighed and Birch Island left. The passengers on the "Evangeline" included Chief Manitowahsing, John Esquimaux, his wife, and mother-in-law.

In a little over two hours they arrived and safely anchored at Little Current Lumber Yard, where the Bishop was glad to find his son ready to relieve him for a while of his responsible duties at the wheel.

The excitement occasioned by the Bishop's visit and the large Indian picnic on Birch Island in time wore away; the Indians returned to their fishing and other occupations, and the missionary to his more arduous labours. As usual during the late autumn and early winter he was obliged to confine his visits chiefly to those of his stations situated on the island. Then when the ice at length became firm and the snow "packed" Mr. Frost got ready his horse and

LITTLE CURRENT LUMBER YARD.

sleigh and visited many of the lumber camps and the more distant of his stations.

So the time passed, and soon the ever welcome festival of Christmas again came round. At St. Andrew's Church in the Indian village of Sheguiandah the Christmas decorations were more than usually elaborate, and greater care had been taken to do the work neatly. The wreaths and festoons were well made, and better taste was shown in the selection of colours, for although the Indians are very fond of a mixture of brilliant hues, they were very ready to be guided by the suggestions of the missionary. When the decorations were completed the women scrubbed the floors and made the church tidy for the Christmas services.

There was a celebration of the Holy Communion at daybreak on Christmas morning, and a large number of Indians, both men and women, were present and communicated. Their demeanour was most reverent, and the few words of counsel, exhortation and encouragement that were spoken by the missionary at the close of the celebration were listened to with earnest attention.

Morning Prayer was said in this church at nine o'clock, when the building was full to overflowing, for all the Indians who had been from home, employed at various places, came back to Sheguiandah for the purpose of being present at the Christmas services. The singing was tuneful and hearty, and

I

the congregation most devout. It would have given the missionary much pleasure to have stayed all day with these earnest Indian Christians, but he was expected to hold four other services in different villages, as well as to conduct Sunday School.

It is customary for the Indians at Sheguiandah to have a great feast on Christmas Day, but Mr. Frost told them that as Christmas Day fell on a Sunday this year, it would be better to postpone their feast to the following day. This suggestion was carried out, and the missionary was invited to be present on the happy occasion. First came the supper, which was such a large affair that all the women in the village had been busily preparing it for some little time beforehand. The dishes included fish and partridges, meats of all kinds, a varied assortment of vegetables, and cakes without number. While supper was in progress some white people arrived and were kindly invited to share the good things provided. Then followed speeches and songs, and Manitowahsing, chief, lay reader and catechist, made a speech that was long after remembered.

On Tuesday evening they had their usual Christmas tree entertainment, when the gifts of clothing sent by the Women's Auxiliary were distributed; two poor widows and their children being especially well provided with useful clothing. It was suggested that some gifts of Indian manufacture should be sent as souvenirs to the ladies of the Women's Auxiliary, a suggestion which was soon afterwards carried out. At Aundagwahmenekauning, a similar entertainment was held on the following Friday; here also, a number of garments were distributed among the Indians.

CHAPTER XVIII.

BURNT OUT.

ONE afternoon in January, 1893, Mr. Frost visited Conlon's camp. In the evening he gave the men working there a sermon, and they in return gave him a bunk for the night. On the following day he spent the whole of the forenoon at the camp amongst the men, who numbered about eighty souls. Here, besides holding the service, the missionary distributed a large number of papers and magazines. After the midday meal he left for another camp, where he proceeded to do as at Conlon's.

On March the Second, Mr. Frost left home to visit the Indians on Spanish river, and as he had to pass near Conlon's camp again he took the opportunity of paying the men another visit. They were delighted to see him, and after supper the cook himself proposed to clear up the common dining room and to arrange it for service. When he had done so a large number of the men who attended the service on the former occasion eagerly took advantage of this second opportunity of worshipping God, leaving their own quarters immediately after the signal agreed upon was given. They hastened to the room that had been prepared, and most earnestly took part in the responses and listened with deep attention to Mr. Frost's address. The missionary again spent the night at the camp, and the next morning proceeded on his journey to minister to the Indians at Spanish River.

By the end of the month Holy Week had returned, and Mr. Frost was very busy holding services each day. On Good Friday and Easter Day the same number of services were held as in former years. Then the roads began to give way, and for a time the missionary had to confine his efforts to narrower limits. However, early in May he was once more able to get further afield.

This month was to bring the mission and its missionary a great trouble, for on the morning of Thursday, May 18th, his house was destroyed by fire. Early that morning the Indians at Sheguiandah were awakened by the lurid light of flames leaping forth from one of the houses in the village. Rushing to the spot they found the missionary's dwelling in flames.

Mr. Frost and his wife were both away at the time but the Indians made every effort to save as much of his property as was possible. Part of the furniture out of one of the rooms on the ground floor was all that could be rescued; all the rest was burnt, and the house reduced to ashes.

The house had only been built a few months before and the requirements of the insurance companies had not yet been complied with, so that neither the building itself nor its contents wer insured. Hence with the exception of the furniture mentioned, the missionary not only lost his house, but everything else, save that which he had with him at the time. Thus both to himself and to his people the accident was most disastrous, all the more distressing as the Parsonage was built after much self-denying effort both on the part of the missionary and the Indians who had helped in its erection.

In a few days Mr. Frost returned home, only to find that the cruel fire had destroyed his home. Overwhelming as this disaster was, yet he was not discouraged, but took up his quarters in a house about a mile or so away on the other side of the Sheguiandah Bay. Here he was within sight of his old house and the Indian village he loved so much. His new abode was a very old house, much dilapidated; but owing to the kindness of friends and to the Women's Auxiliary, it was furnished with a fair amount of comfort, and here the summer and winter months were spent. The Bishop did not think it would be wise to commence rebuilding the Parsonage till sufficient money was in hand for its completion lest the work should come to a standstill for want of funds.

Meanwhile the work of the mission was carried on just as before. One of the missionary's vehicles was burnt, but he was able to buy another to replace it. The four services each Sunday were held with the same regularity, although his being at a greater distance from the churches made the undertaking more difficult for the missionary. However, the new abode on the bay afforded a good moorage for Mr. Frost's boat, of which during the summer he made good use, frequently visiting the Indian villages on the mainland. But these trips were not without their difficulties and disappointments.

Once when visiting one of these villages, a lake some two miles in length had to be crossed. Being unable to use his sail boat, Mr. Frost borrowed a large heavy canoe, and with the help of an Indian, carried it for some distance to the edge of the lake. After paddling a few yards great was the disappointment felt by him when the canoe began to fill rapidly with water, and turning immediately, Mr. Frost had barely time to reach the shore before being swamped.

However he discovered an old punt which carried him safely over the lake, and, after great difficulties in finding his way through the bush and over the rocks, he at length reached the village. Here the Indians gave him a good supper, after which a hearty service was held in the church which was attended by a large congregation.

Sometimes great disappointment is caused when, after a long and troublesome journey, the missionary finds the village almost deserted; yet while the Indians are so wandering in their habits and mode of life, this can hardly be prevented. Although often disappointed in this way, the missionary has many opportunities of ministering, for if not at the villages, the Indians are to be found at different places of encampment in the neighbourhood, where there are often several families assembled together. The Indians now make better boats than formerly, and a large number have tents which are an improvement upon the old birch-bark wigwams.

The weather which had hitherto been beautiful, now changed, and many times in the course of his duties was Mr. Frost compelled to face wind, and rain, and storms. Frequently would he arrive at some camp after a toilsome journey drenched by the rain. and then he would have to sit by the camp fire partly clothed while the rest of his things were drying on the stakes above the fire. But when they were dried there would usually be an excellent supper provided, and often a comfortable night's rest was obtainable.

A WIGWAM.

CHAPTER XIX.

AN INDIAN FUNERAL.

One evening during the summer the missionary arrived at an Indian village and was disappointed to find that the majority of its inhabitants were away from home. However, on the shore near the spot where he had moored his boat, he found an Indian called Big John, who had encamped there with his family. Big John belonged to a neighbouring village and was one of the missionary's flock, so Mr. Frost was glad to go and speak to him and his wife.

He enquired of them after the health of a little child who had been very ill, and whom the missionary had lately been visiting. Big John said that the child had died the previous day, and that he had been helping to make the coffin and assisting in the preparations for the funeral, which was to take place on the morrow. "It is good that you came," he continued, "or otherwise we should have had no black coat to perform the rites and prayers of burial." John then helped the missionary to set up his tent, and brought his blankets and rugs from the boat.

The missionary then set forth to visit his bereaved friends, who lived at some little distance from the shore. He found them in their cabin, intently watching the dead child in its coffin. The corpse was beautifully dressed, and had been laid out with great care by the fond parents, who had probably spent all their savings on the decoration of their dear child's body. The missionary stayed with them for some little time and made arrangements for the customary service of song in the evening, promising to come and help with the singing, and to speak some words of instruction and consolation.

The Indians are accustomed to sit up with their bereaved friends on the night preceding a funeral, passing the time in prayer and singing hymns. It was to one of these gatherings that the missionary promised to return. In the meantime the chief and his family arrived, and also two or three others, some from considerable distances, and among them some of the relations of the child. At the appointed time they all assembled and held a very lengthy meeting. About twenty hymns were sung at intervals, and Mr. Frost filled up these intervals by reading passages from the Bible which speak of the Christian's hope in the resurrection and belief in a future life, afterwards explaining these truths and consoling the weeping parents. It was midnight when he left his friends and sought rest in his own tent.

At nine o'clock on the following morning, the first part of the funeral service was held in the little church, and was attended by all the inhabitants of the village, save those who were engaged in the distant camps. The service over, they repaired to the graveyard, which was at some distance from the church. The parents of the child and some friends accompanied the little coffin in a boat, the missionary and some others walking through the woods, arriving soon after the former had reached the graveyard. Now Indians are very deliberate in all their movements, and especially so at funerals, so when the missionary arrived at the graveyard he found no grave had been dug; only a few preparations had been made for commencing it.

As this would be a matter of time, the Chief, fearing that Mr. Frost would find it very wearisome to stand about while the grave was being dug, suggested that he should take a gun and amuse himself by shooting partridges. There were six stalwart Indians engaged to dig the little grave, which was only about three feet long, and the soil was sandy and soft, but they worked very slowly. Again the missionary was advised to amuse himself with shooting, but he said he would stay with them and help dig, lest darkness should overtake them before the grave was completed.

When they had reached to a depth of three feet, Big John undertook to dig, but he could not move to work. After a few helpless and hopeless efforts he withdrew from the grave, and another man of slighter build jumped in and worked for a time. Then another took his place, and several laboured at it before a depth of five feet was reached.

At last the work was done, but then another difficulty arose. The shell—a rough kind of case which is placed in the grave and into which the coffin is lowered—was not yet made; and, worse still, no one had remembered to bring a saw. But an Indian does not often find himself in such a fix that he does not know how to extricate himself. So on the present occasion some one suggested that an axe would do to cut off some lengths of boarding for the shell. So the axe was tried and found to answer.

Then it was discovered that there were no nails for fastening the boards together. The missionary felt in his pockets and found two nails, and an Indian produced three more. The chief thought that with care these might be made to do, and very soon the shell was finished and fitted into the grave.

While the men had thus been engaged in working at the grave the women had lighted a fire some distance away and were cooking supper, and just as the proceedings at the grave had arrived at the stage of completion, the announcement was made that supper was ready.

In vain did the missionary entreat that the funeral should first be finished before supper was eaten. But the Indians were obdurate, and contended that as everything was cooked and ready, it would be better to have supper first, the dead, they said, "were in no hurry."

As there was no shaking their resolution the missionary had to give away, and he followed the Indians to the place where supper had been prepared. There were many kinds of vegetables, fish, meat, and a dish called "Indian Choke Dog," but perhaps the missionary would have been better pleased if he had been provided with a spoon or fork, or even a plate, for the Indians had forgotten to bring these necessary articles. Yet this was a funeral, not a picnic, and all the time the little coffin had been lying in the boat, thither the Indians now went.

The missionary put on his surplice, and a procession was formed to the grave. After the service a hymn was sung and the missionary gave a short address, telling them how David, when he was bereaved, had said "I shall go to Him, but He shall not return to me." The parents thanked him warmly and said they were glad he had come in time to give their dear child the privilege of Christian burial. The funeral had occupied the whole of the long summer's day. When they reached the village

> Nox erat, et coelo fulgebat luna sereno
> Inter minora sidera. HOR. EPOD. XV.

flooding with her passionless radiance the dwellings of the living and the dead.

CHAPTER XX.

SAW-MILLS.

The lumber interest is carried on very extensively on the north shore of the Georgian Bay, opposite the Great Manitoulin Island. Here the land is extremely rocky and the hills are covered with timber, chiefly pine. Around these hills are valleys and ravines of considerable extent, in which also the pine trees grow and have been growing for centuries. Amongst the hills are many small lakes mostly connected by small rivers or creeks, thus forming a highway for the lumberman. Through them he sends his logs to the larger lakes where they can be towed to a mill by a tug or steamboat. The work of cutting down timber is commenced in September or the latter end of August.

When a "limit" or timber berth—which has already been described—has been secured, a suitable spot is selected on which to build a shanty—a large rough building of logs, roofed in either with logs or with boards covered with shingle or tarred felt to keep out the rain. It is furnished with bunks for sleeping and a large stove for heating purposes.

Then another somewhat similar shanty is built for the cook, in which the meals are prepared and eaten, and which forms a sort of common dining room for the camp. It should be mentioned that lately considerable advancement has been made in the accommodation and furnishing of lumber camps with regard both to the sleeping and other apartments. Not many years ago the arrangements were far more primitive and far less comfortable than they are now; formerly there used to be a large open fire in the centre of the camp, and the smoke made its way through the roof, while if there were any wind, it spread through the shanty, nearly suffocating the inmates. Now this is done away with and a stove takes its place. There is also a considerable improvement in the cooking.

Near the sleeping and dining camp a stable is built for the horses, a shop for the blacksmith and carpenter, and a smaller building for an office in which the provisions are kept. This building is commonly called the " van," and serves as an office for the clerk and a sleeping place for the master of the camp, called the " boss." Here also the missionary is sometimes lodged when he visits the camp. Such then are the buildings erected for the use of the men working on the " limit."

We have already seen how the logs are conveyed down the river to the mill where they are sawn into planks or made into shingles. These mills are usually of wood built upon a stone foundation, and are one or more storeys in height. When the logs have reached the saw-mill they are placed in a boom, and, as required, drawn up from the river on an inclined plane. On arriving at the top of the plane they are rolled on to a moveable bed or carriage which runs over a tramway fixed upon the floor of the mill.

Below this tramway there is a frame in which a circular saw is fixed and which is secured to the foundations of the mill. The carriage is provided with a rack and a lever, and is so connected with the machinery driving the saw that the log is sent forward at exactly the same rate as the saw cuts; and, in less time than it takes to write these words, a rough log may be cut up into inch boards. First, one outside slab is taken off, then another, until four have been removed. The log is now square and is ready to be cut into boards. The carriage is then placed so that the saw will cut a board of the required thickness, and when the lever is applied, it is drawn over the tramway, thus bringing the log into contact with the saw, and a board is cut off. It is then run back again, and the process repeated with such rapidity that several men are required to carry the boards to the trucks waiting for them. As soon as a load is completed it is removed, and the boards stacked with great regularity in the yard without, to await sale or shipment.

Shingle mills are often, but not always attached to a saw-mill. These mills work very much upon the same principle as those for cutting up logs. Shingles are made from what are called shingle bolts—trunks

A SAW-MILL

of pine trees cut into lengths of four feet and split longitudinally into four or more pieces. These are first prepared by being cut up into three equal lengths, the surface being cut level, and are then ready for the shingle saw.

When the saw has done its work the shingle is a smooth piece of board, sixteen inches long, of uniform width, nearly half an inch thick at one end and regularly tapering to nothing at the other. As the shingles drop from the machine they fall down an inclined plane at the foot of which are a number of boys who pack them into frames which are constructed to hold exactly two hundred and fifty. These frames are fastened with hoop iron and the shingles are now ready for shipment. Shingles are largely used for roofing buildings and in some cases outside walls are covered with them.

The work, whether in the camp, on the drive, or in the mill, is at all times both laborious and dangerous. In the bush, time and again men lose their lives by some untimely accident, aggravated by the want of surgical skill and proper nursing. An accident happens; the camp is many miles from the nearest town; the injured man has to be carried as best he may; and every now and then some poor fellow dies from sheer exhaustion on the way.

Then in the mill, an accident may, and frequently does happen. One of the saws will split or some of the machinery give way and pieces of iron or steel are hurled with terrible force in every direction. Woe to the man whom such a piece may chance to strike; his body will, in all probability, be carried from the building lifeless.

Then again there are dangers from fire. Year by year lumber to the value of many thousands of dollars is consumed by this destructive enemy. The engine shaft is a prolific cause of danger in this respect; a spark unnoticed may rest upon the roof, which in nearly every case is of shingles, and in a short space of time the whole place is in flames. Everything which human foresight can devise to prevent a mishap of this nature is provided. Guards are placed upon the top of the shaft, and large barrels, full of water, are kept in readiness upon a platform erected in the ridge of the roof. In a word no precaution is omitted, but too often all are without avail.

CHAPTER XXI.

Among Lumbermen.

During the winter Mr. Frost took a tour for a fortnight to the distant parts of his mission. Leaving Sheguiandah early one morning, he started for Killarney, travelling over the ice which was fairly good, with the exception of numerous cracks. Sometimes it was necessary for him to get out of his sleigh and try the ice with an axe to see where it was best to cross the track, since on some ice there are spaces of open water concealed by a drift of snow and sufficiently large to engulf both missionary and horse. On arriving at Killarney he called on those who were members of the church and held small gatherings for prayer and reading.

A pleasant drive of twenty-three miles brought the missionary to Beaverstone, where he was well received. Arriving in the evening he met several of his old friends, who were collected together at the office, and in an adjoining shanty he discovered an old man who had been the first to greet him when he visited the camp many years before. There was one young man, who had recently come out from England, and who had met with an accident which confined him to the camp for two or three days.

The missionary was much interested in him, and had many opportunities of conversing with him, and giving him advice which might be useful to him in his new and untried life. Mr. Frost was encouraged by the success of the service which he held in this camp, but disappointed in the singing, scarcely anyone being able to join with him in the hymns.

On leaving Beaverstone the missionary travelled ten miles through the woods to his next destination, Bad River. The journey was agreeable and the landscape varied. Part of the woods consisted of dense groves of pine and spruce; then came a grove of fine white birches, their shining silvery bark forming a striking contrast to the dense pine woods just passed. The missionary was disappointed on reachin Bad River to find that an old friend whom he had known for many years was not at the camp. His children, however, were very attentive and endeavoured to make up for their father's absence.

The clerk in charge made the necessary arrangements, and the usual service was held; a great contrast in respect to the singing to that held at the last camp visited. Here the men joined heartily and actually possessed hymn books of their own. Mr. Frost slept in the office, and next day pushed on to Beaver Meadow Camp.

On the way, he saw from the stains in the snow, that some hunter had been killing deer and had dragged their carcases over the snow; there were some wolves also in the neighbourhood, but fortunately they did not attack him. When he arrived the men were working in the woods, but in the evening they came into the camp and attended the services, Afterwards Mr. Frost showed some views from a magic lantern which he had with him. The cook in this camp was a native of England and it was pleasant to see how keenly interested he was in the affairs of the old country.

McDonald's Camp, the next visited, was entirely different to the others. It was built on a swamp of tameracks; the company was larger and more varied; the men were of many different nationalities, and of diverse occupations before they came to the woods. One had been a sailor, and had met the manager of the camp in Toronto, and had taken work in the woods not knowing at all what it was like. The missionary was especially interested in some English people who were thinking of settling on a farm in the north-west of Canada. The foreman and his wife and family with many others were present at the service, and so much interest was evinced that Mr. Frost was prevailed on to stay over Sunday and give them a Sunday morning service.

On Sunday afternoon the missionary drove to the depôt at Beaverstone and held a service there. He then proceeded to Collin's Inlet, being advised not to take his horse, as the ice in the channel was not sufficiently strong to bear one. A couple of dogs were used to draw the sleigh, and the journey was accomplished in safety. Here he spent the night, and next morning returned to the depôt for his horse. But the rain had come on, and the water in the river had risen to such a degree that the dogs were almost swimming. The sleigh was abandoned, and the missionary made his way along the bank, plunging through the deep snow.

The journey through the woods to Point Gromline was not so unpleasant, and Mr. Frost was warmly welcomed by the Indians who live in that village. The houses here are rather better than the general run of Indian cabins, some indeed being quite superior. The missionary first went to see an old friend whose name was John Kahgahgum. John conducted Mr. Frost to his father's house where he said there was a better place to put the horse. Here the missionary was very comfortably lodged, and in the evening preached to the Indians in their own tongue.

The following day was very wet, so the missionary was obliged to stay in the village for yet another day, in the meantime visiting from house to house. The Indians promised to make him a handsome pair of beaded mocassins, as an acknowledgment of the appreciation with which they received his visits.

The missionary then returned to Collin's Inlet and was there informed that the men at Gray's Lake would be glad to have a visit from him. So he set

LUMBERMEN.

out for that place, accompanied by one of his Indian friends on the most difficult parts of the route, and afterwards making his way through the woods alone. The travelling was very bad because the thaw had raised the water in the rivers and marshes making it very difficult to get along. The water in places reached up to the horse's flank.

At length he arrived at his destination, and was well received; the master of the camp exerting himself to make the service a success. Most of the men here came from Eastern Ontario, close on the borders of Quebec. The missionary was so pleased with the success of this visit that he determined to go on to the next camp at Long Lake.

During the night a slight frost congealed the water in a marsh through which he had to pass on the way to Long Lake. But the ice was not sufficiently strong to bear the horse, and every step it broke through, and for over a mile the poor creature had to wade through a mixture of ice and water. Consequently when the camp was reached the animal was nearly exhausted with the cold and fatigue. The men in the camp were prevented from working owing to the floods, so service was commenced early in the evening.

Next morning Mr. Frost returned towards Collin's Inlet which he reached after a long and troublesome journey. On his way to Sheguiandah he visited Manitowaning and held a service in that place as well as a celebration of the Holy Communion.

CHAPTER XXII.

A Wedding.

We in England, when we wish to see a clergyman have but two or three miles at the most to travel and can usually find him at any given time, can but little understand the hardships which have often to be undergone by others, seeking his services, in distant lands. Not unfrequently a distance of thirty or forty miles has to be travelled before the place at which the nearest clergyman resides can be reached.

Then, if he happens to be away from home visiting some of the distant stations of his mission, there may be days of waiting and anxious delay, and on some occasions it may be necessary to dispatch a second and more urgent messenger. In England, too, it is usual to give reasonable notice before a clergyman is expected to perform the marriage ceremony. In by far the greater number of instances in Canada no banns are published, but a license is procured from the nearest magistrate, or other person authorized to issue them, on the production of which the local clergyman proceeds to unite the happy pair.

Hence a clergyman is often called upon to officiate without previous warning, and that sometimes at the most unusual and inconvenient hours. But even when this is not the case much delay and anxiety are often caused by the great distances that have sometimes to be travelled.

It may be interesting to give an account of a wedding taken by the Rev. J. H. McLeod, the clergyman in charge of Gore Bay. Not long ago Mr. McLeod promised to officiate at Meldrum Bay, a distance of sixty-five miles, by road, from Gore Bay. The time allowed to reach this spot was nearly two days, and as the wedding took place on the Tuesday, the missionary left his house on the Monday morning; the time of year was late winter, the snow was already beginning to disappear from some parts of the ground, and the ice was thin and worn by the heavy rains. The vehicle used was a sleigh drawn by two strong young ponies, and well indeed was it that they were strong, for the first ten miles of their journey led over very bad roads, the surface of which was rough bare ground, with no snow on which the sleigh might run.

When the missionary approached the ice matters did not improve much, for at about half a mile from the shore the surface of the ice was found to be covered with water to the depth of a foot. Having heard that the ice was safe, Mr. McLeod decided to venture across it, although a gale of wind which was blowing at the time made the passage still more disagreeable. After a drive of twenty miles during which three dangerous cracks in the ice had to be crossed, the shore was happily reached, and a further drive of three miles on land brought the missionary to the house of a friend where he had arranged to halt and spend the night.

Here he met with a very kind reception, and after partaking of refreshments, he set out on foot to visit a place about three miles distant, accompanied by the son of his host, where he baptised several children. He had hoped to hold a service in the neighbourhood, but this had to be abandoned as the roads were nearly impassable. In the evening he walked back to his friend's house, which was reached only with difficulty owing to the darkness and the soft state of the road.

> Nor even moon nor stars display,
> Through the dark shade, one guiding ray
> To show the perils of the way.
>
> ROBERT SOUTHEY.

It was necessary to make an early start on the following morning as the missionary had still a long drive before him. The snow, which was soft before was rendered still softer by a steady downfall of rain during the night. However, after an early breakfast, a start was made notwithstanding the rain which was still falling, for when the object of a journey is a wedding, it would never do to disappoint the young people.

For the first thirteen miles the road was extremely rough, indeed it would have been a hard matter to find its equal, even in the Muskoka district or the Rocky Mountains. It had been decided to travel the whole distance by the road, but when Sheshewanese Bay was reached, Mr. McLeod changed his mind and determined to risk the twenty miles' drive on the ice to Meldrum Bay: once on the ice again the ponies advanced at a good pace and the travelling was fair, with the exception of a few cracks in the ice.

Shortly after rounding the last point going into Meldrum Bay, some five miles distant, the sleigh was sighted by some of the expectant and anxious people, who soon announced, to the great delight of all, and expecially of the young people about to be married, that the missionary was coming. In about half an hour's time after rounding the point, Mr. McLeod arrived at his destination, none the worse for his long and fatiguing journey. He was warmly welcomed by the people of the village, and his ponies were taken to a comfortable stable where they were well fed and cared for.

At five o'clock in the evening the marriage ceremony was performed. Afterwards a most excellent dinner was provided to about eighty guests. The tables were then cleared and many games and amusements indulged in by the younger people. The next day, Wednesday, the missionary visited in the village and immediate neighbourhood and baptized a child. In the evening another wedding took place and amusements kept up until a late hour, brought what was quite a festive time at Meldrum Bay to a close.

On Thursday Mr. McLeod made an early start for Gore Bay having decided to run the risk of the ice all the way down rather than attempt the roads. He reached home in the afternoon having made a short stop at Cape Robert's Lighthouse. The ponies went willingly, and no accident or misfortune befel them or their driver on the way. The whole population of Gore Bay were unanimous in welcoming their clergyman home again and congratulating him on his safe return. Some said they would not have undertaken that journey for fifty dollars, and others asserted that on no consideration would they have been induced to expose themselves to such risk. A few days after Mr. McLeod's return, a team of horses and a team of four dogs were drowned on this same route.

CHAPTER XXIII.

Conclusion.

Thus have we briefly traced some of the church's work among the Ojibway Indians and lumbermen in one part of the missionary diocese of Algoma during a period of nearly five years—from Advent, 1889; and my task is nearly done. Much that is both interesting and valuable has been left unsaid, more for the reason that my object has been to produce a simple sketch than for any other. But before we bid adieu to the great Manitoulin and its faithful workers, it would be well perhaps to enquire somewhat as to other missions in the diocese.

Perhaps a future writer will give a full account of them; we will content ourselves with asking if they are all like those which we have been considering. Those who have read " Life in Algoma " will readily understand that such is not the case. But others may not have the opportunity of reading that little book, and for their information it is here stated that Algoma has within its borders missions differing more widely from one another than parishes differ from each other in England, even if the contrast be between town and country parishes.

For instance there is one mission which contains two villages distant from each other some two hundred and fifty miles. Both villages are on the Canadian Pacific Railway and on the north shore of Lake Superior. They have to be content with services on alternate Sundays as it is impossible for the missionary to be at both places on the same day. Then it will be asked, what do the people do who live between these points.

The answer is, the clergyman gives them as much of his time as he can spare on a week-day. His means of travel is of course the railway, and in the course of the year he travels some 13,000 miles. Another mission stretches for one hundred and twenty miles on the Algoma branch of the same line of railway, the conditions being somewhat similar to those in the former case.

Then there are a few small towns and villages such as Bracebridge, Gravenhurst, Fort William, Huntsville, North Bay, Parry Sound, Port Arthur, Sault Ste Marie, and Sudbury; still smaller villages and hamlets as Aspdin, Burke's Falls, Hilton, Ilfracombe, Port Carling, Rosseau, Schreiber, and Uffington. All of these are inhabited by a white population, to a large extent settlers from the old country or their descendants.

Then besides these there are other missions such as Garden River and Neepigon, where the population is either partly or entirely Indian. At each of the places mentioned there is a resident clergyman; but in none save those which are self-supporting, can he devote his undivided energies to that place. In all other cases the clergyman has from one to three or more out-stations clusted around his central head-quarters, and separated from it by from six to ten miles.

As a rule each missionary has three services on a Sunday, thus often having to eat "in haste" as the Israelites did the Passover. For this reason nearly all the Sunday Schools are more or less in the hands of the laity. The general character of the population may be regarded as most encouraging. There is just the same degree of culture and refinement, and therefore of congenial association and companionship which is met with in communities in England of a like size, where the people are all actively engaged in their several callings.

In most of the towns and villages there are usually beside the clergyman, one or more lawyers and doctors, and of course the usual number of tradesmen; but none of them have much more leisure than suffices for their social evening recreation. Outside the centres in the rural districts, the people almost without exception earn their bread by the sweat of their brow, only too thankful in many cases to accomplish even this.

They are for the most part a shrewd, intelligent and industrious people; in manner somewhat independent; in spirit democratic, though thoroughly loyal to England and their English political connection; and they are hospitable to a fault. Let a clergyman go among them, taking them just as he finds them, and accepting what they offer him whether bed or board, he will soon gain a strong hold upon them. Their churchmanship is often the weak point, owing largely to the slenderness of the thread which too often links them to the church. Of church history or thought or distinctive usage they know next to nothing.

Here and there it is refreshing to meet with a staunch supporter of the church, whose creed is intelligent enough to be able to give a rational account of itself. But in the vast majority of cases their churchmanship is merely an hereditary entail, or the result of inter-marriage, or the growth of a liking for an individual clergyman, or perhaps proportioned in an inverse ratio to the distance from the church. Hence the attachment is precarious and easily affected by the course of events. The clergyman is to them the embodiment of the church; if he represents her worthily by his energy, faithfulness and good sense, he will hold them fast while he remains. If he be careless, indifferent or inconsistent, they will soon absent themselves altogether, or drift into one of the many dissenting bodies whose doors stand invitingly open for their admission.

But to return to Manitoulin. At Gore Bay Mr. McLeod and his energetic wife are busy. The missionary with his plans, his specifications and his bills of quantities; the missionary's wife and their people are doing all that in them lies to complete their church, hoping to have it ready for the Bishop to open when he next pays his annual visit. Nor do they forget the higher privileges of their church while thus pushing forward this great temporal work; but, on the contrary, as the one grows so does the other, and both works are alike bearing fruit, each in its own degree.

And Mr. Frost, what of him? Well, he is busy preparing his candidates for confirmation; with his almost unending travels, first among his Indians, then among the lumbermen near home, and anon paying visits to remote and isolated dwellers in more distant parts of his large field, striving to follow in the footsteps of his Divine Master, sacrificing himself that he may serve even the most insignificant of that Master's flock.

And interesting letters from the old diocese come to the late missionary's study in the old land; and to him they come like the bugle call to the old warhorse, and make him long once more to be in the ranks of the pioneer band, and stand shoulder to shoulder with them in the Master's service. But the Church's great Head has other duties and responsibilities for him, therefore he may not choose for himself. Let him then learn to submit without a murmur to His all-seeing wisdom, and to be content with doing what he can, amid his ever-increasing work, for the advancement of the Church in distant lands.

And the Bishop who has sacrificed so much for his diocese, continues " in journeyings oft." Time after time has his strength given way. Again and again has he been warned, yet still he goes on, ever journeying from place to place, now with the white man, now with the red. Sometimes in burning sun; anon with the the thermometer 40° below zero; at the helm of his steamer, with the sun burning the skin and flesh from his face. Again in the winter, subjected to its icy blast, on one occasion so nearly frozen that, having crawled to the house of Rural Dean Llwydd, he was scarcely recognised by the inmates.

In July, of 1894, he paid a visit to the Indians at Negwenenang and Neepigon, travelling in the most primitive manner under the care of Chief Oshkapkida. The journey involved carrying all the provisions required on the way, both going and returning, not excluding bedding and tent. For from the moment he left the railway station, which is seventy miles beyond Port Arthur, he could hope for no supplies until he returned to it again, save that which might fall to the gun or rod. The river Neepigon, up which he had to canoe, is itself forty miles long. On his return journey he reached Port William at noon, Sunday, July 29th, holding service on steamer just before landing.

"IN JOURNEYINGS OFT."

CONCLUSION.

On August 11th he was on his way to pay his annual visit to the Great Manitoulin Island, after which, before the autumn was ended, he visited missions in Parry Sound and Muskoka. Comment is needless, and any words of mine in praise of one whose life is one of such heroic self-sacrifice would be out of place.

> Quae cura patrum, quaeve Quiritium,
> Plenis honorum muneribus tuas,
> Auguste, virtutes in aevum
> Per titulos memoresque fastos
> Aeternet?   HOR. CARM. iv. 14.

The Lamb's Book of Life enshrines those " Inscriptions and retentive annals," and the Resurrection Morn will tell that among the many acts of heroism which the present century has witnessed, not the least are due to the noble band of men and women who gladly give themselves a willing sacrifice, in order that they may carry the message of the Gospel to those who either know not God or are in danger of forgetting him.

The crown which they shall wear eternally shall shine only brighter than the Cross, placed upon the forehead of every Christian babe in baptism, and which upon many an unknown saintly head, now fighting the battle of the Cross, becomes more radient in his Master's eyes, as day by day self is more completely forgotten in self-sacrifice. Well indeed may we thank Him who ruleth over all for having raised up such examples among us.

And the "Evangeline," what of her? She is still in the service of the King of kings; and the lonely fisherman watches, with his boat ready to push off at the first sight of her funnel, so that from her stern the episcopal hand may toss into it a bundle of magazines and papers; which he, in his life attended with so much peril, amid the wonders of the deep, values all the more highly as the years roll by, and as, from his associations and from what he reads, he learns to reverence, more and more deeply, Him who created all.

THE END.

IN THE PRESS.

BY THE SAME AUTHOR.

Crown 8vo., Stiff Covers, Published in Parts, price 1/4 each.*

Addresses

ON

St. Matthew's Gospel.

These plain and simple addresses were originally delivered in the Dioceses of London and Algoma, afterwards at Cambridge and other places in the Diocese of Ely.

They have been carefully revised, and are now published by request, more especially for the use of Lay-Preachers and others residing in isolated places and in distant lands.

PART I. READY IN AUGUST.

* Copies for use in Algoma and other Missionary Dioceses, may be procured at reduced rates, on application to the Author, through the Publishers.

LONDON:
THOMAS BROWN & CO.,
9, RAY STREET, FARRINGDON ROAD, E.C.

IN PREPARATION

BY THE SAME AUTHOR

𝔇𝔢𝔡𝔦𝔠𝔞𝔱𝔢𝔡 𝔱𝔬 𝔥𝔦𝔰 𝔊𝔯𝔞𝔠𝔢 𝔱𝔥𝔢

Lord Archbishop of Canterbury.

CROWN 8VO.,

ARTISTIC CLOTH BINDING AND PAPER COVERS.

DUTY'S CALL,

A Story of a girl's sacrifice in the service of others, with some brief sketches of undergraduate life.

READY IN THE AUTUMN.

BY THE SAME AUTHOR.

Crown 8vo. Artistic Cloth Binding. Illustrated. Price 2s.

"LIFE IN ALGOMA."

SOME PRESS NOTICES.

" . . . . . It is written in a frank and simple style, and the writer shows no boastfulness in relating the story of the hard work which he did or the privations which he endured, because he believes that he was just doing his duty. . . . . HIS BRIGHT LITTLE NARRATIVE DESERVES A PLACE AMONG THE BEST MISSIONARY LITERATURE OF THE CHURCH."—*The Guardian.*

" A deeply-moving record which we have read from cover to cover, well illustrated and giving an idea of life in Algoma, that shows its interest and its difficulties. We recommend all interested in Colonial life to read the book."—*Church Bells.*

" It is a brilliant, vivid and deeply interesting account of a missionary clergyman's life. . . . We have seldom read a more delightful volume."—*Scot's Magazine.*

" . . . . . A very vivid picture of a clergyman's life and work. . . . The sketches of Canadian life are of an exceedingly interesting nature, and not a little part of the merit of the book lies in the artistic illustrations."—*Sussex Daily News.*

" A very interesting narrative of three years of a clergyman's life and Church work in that diocese. . . *Sunday School Chronicle.*

SOME PRESS NOTICES

". . . . An interesting account of a clergyman's life and work in a diocese of the wilderness. . . . . The record of missionary labour is varied by interesting descriptions of border life. . . ."—*Manchester Guardian.*

" ' Life in Algoma ' will be read with much interest."
The Rock.

". . . . . Life in Algoma by a clergyman who endeavours to hide his identity under the initials of H.N.B. . . . gives in an unpretentious manner some accounts of the trials, difficulties and successes of a faithful pastor, and some pleasant and touching instances of the eager self-denial of the people in order to obtain the ministrations of their beloved Church."—*Liverpool Courier.*

". . . . . a most interesting story of three years' faithful work amidst the villages and outlying houses of one part of the great diocese of Algoma. No true Churchman can read this account without his interest being increased in this branch of the Church's work, and we trust also in the two great Societies which most help to carry it on."—*The National Church.*

". . . . Especially acceptable to those interested in mission work. . . . Written in a frank and simple style, showing no egotism, but giving true and stirring sketches of Canadian life, with pleasant and touching instances of eager self-denial of the people in order that they may secure the ministrations of the Church. . . . This charming little book deserves a high place among the missionary literature of the English Church."—*Cambridge Chronicle and University Journal.*

". . . . Very prettily written, and makes one almost long to visit the portions of the country described. . . . . . Makes very evident what might be done if there were only the men to do it."—*Canadian Church Magazine and Mission News.*

"If more of the books written with the same object in view as this one is intended to serve contained as much instruction, given as interestingly, much more would be accomplished by means of missionary literature. . . . Coming fresh from the old land, the peculiar features of the new struck the Author with unusual force, and he sets down with remarkable vividness his first impressions. He gives a charming account of his ministrations among the people, of his difficulties, of his success, of the excellent character of the settlers, and the desire they have for the message which he bore them."—*The Globe* (Toronto).

". . . . A very true and life-like picture of a clergyman's difficulties, even when he is sympathetic and successful."
—*Canadian Churchman*.

". . . . . A very interesting account, told in simple and unaffected language. The work of a missionary, the part the people take in all Church effort, the character of the country and its prospects are all described. The illustrations are good and add interest to the book. . . " Life in Algoma " will no doubt be added to many Sunday School libraries."—*Evangelical Churchman*.

". . . . . Tells of life in the midst of pioneer settlers in a way that must interest and instruct the English reader. . . . . At some future day, when a history of this Missionary Diocese is written, the pages before us will be drawn upon for many facts."—*Algoma Missionary News*.

Writing to the *Algoma Association Paper*, January, 1895, The Bishop speaks of "Life in Algoma" being better understood, thanks to the book published under that title.

London :

A. T. Roberts, Son & Co.,
5, Hackney Road, N.E.

www.ingramcontent.com/pod-product-compliance
Lightning Source LLC
Chambersburg PA
CBHW031452160426
43195CB00010BB/950